# Gifts to Cross Stitch

B.J. McDonald

# Acknowledgments

I sincerely appreciate all the support from the cross stitch companies listed in the Resources section, the contributing designers with their wonderful creative talents, my dear friend Julie Stephani for making this book possible, photographer Bob Best for all his hard work, page designer Donna Mummery and cover designer Marilyn McGrane for the beautiful design inside and out, and my editor Maria Turner for her patience and skill to bring the fruits of everyone's labor in the book to a great finished product.

Published by

krause publications
An F&W Publications Company

700 East State Street • Iola, WI 54990-0001
715-445-2214 • 888-457-2873
www.krause.com

Please call or write for our free catalog of publications. Our toll-free number to place an order or obtain a free catalog is (800) 258-0929.

Printed in China.

Library of Congress Catalog Number: 2003108020
ISBN: 0-87349-640-X

Editor: Maria Turner
Book Design: Donna Mummery

# Introduction

Recently, I helped my mother clean her closet and came across numerous boxes of keepsakes she had collected over the years. Within one of the boxes was my first counted cross stitch piece. The project was pathetic. It was so thick and matted on the back that it could have been used as a rug! How could I have ever been proud of it? But in my mother's eyes, it was a beautiful treasure.

My daughter tackled her first cross stitch project when she was only four years old. Like my mother, there were no imperfections in this mother's eyes when my daughter presented me with her treasure. It's a keepsake I shall always cherish.

There's no better way to commemorate a special occasion than with a cross stitch project. Anyone can go buy a gift from a store, but a cross stitch gift takes on a more personal touch because of the time and love invested in making the keepsake.

As a cross stitcher, you are a lot like a painter. You start with a blank canvas (fabric) and "paint" your design with needle and thread. When the design is completed, it is a masterpiece simply because you stitched it. The project has your heart and soul lovingly woven in each stitch.

You don't have to wait for a special occasion to stitch a gift. I have proudly displayed a stitched gift from my dear friend Vonda for more than 20 years. Its simple design and verse, "Thank you for being you," has a powerful and inspiring message. It is a constant reminder of how precious our friendship is.

Then there's the beautiful tray my friend Peggy made for me. It's a reminder of the wonderful times spent with her teaching me how to cross stitch. Some stitched pieces are from friends who have passed on—but their memories live on through their needlework.

The projects in this book are primarily stitched on prefinished items so that when you finish the stitching, you already will have a completed gift. However, many of the designs can be stitched for matting and framing if you choose to do so. For example, if you have a star football player, you can stitch only the football from the Sports Afghan and have it framed. The mouse pad designs, Frosty Folks, Whimsical Santas, Flower-of-the-Month, Poppy and Daisy Wreath, and many more can be stitched for framing instead of on the prefinished items shown within. The ideas are endless when you use your imagination!

Your stitched projects do not have to be "perfect" to bring pleasure to someone—including yourself. So what if you have a few mistakes? I promise you that the majority of people will not know and even if they know, they will not care. So relax and be happy with what you stitch.

Start stitching some memories today…for tomorrow's heirlooms.

Happy stitching,

*Bj. McDonald*

# Table of Contents

# General Instructions

## Fabric

For your first counted cross stitch project, you should choose a fabric with a thread count that you can easily see. Fourteen-count fabric is excellent for a beginner. As you learn more about counted cross stitch, you can then try finer fabrics that have more threads to the inch. The higher the thread count, the finer the fabric and thus the more challenging to stitch.

Counted cross stitch is worked on an evenweave fabric that has the same number of threads woven vertically (warp) and horizontally (weft).

Counted thread (cross stitch) means you must count the fabric threads (linen) or thread squares (Aida) as you stitch. Evenweave fabrics are available in a variety of colors, fiber content, thread counts, and weave patterns.

Aida is the most popular fabric for cross stitching because of its easy-to-see squares. Aida is woven in a complex weave of groups of four threads that form distinctive squares with corner holes. It is great for beginners. Aida is available in various colors and counts: 6-, 7- (Country Aida), 8-, 10- (primarily damask Aidas), 11-, 14-, 16-, and 18-counts.

Hardanger, available in 100 percent cotton, 100 percent linen, and 100 percent wool, is a 22-count evenweave that can also be used for cross stitch as well as hardanger.

Linen is another popular fabric choice for cross stitch. Linen is a plain-weave fabric that means each fabric thread is woven in the typical over-under method. At the time of this book's production, the lowest linen count was 16-count (from Wichelt Imports) ranging to 55-count (from Zweigart). Charles Craft also has a 20-count linen. The most widely used linen counts are 25-count Dublin, 28-count Cashel, 32-count Belfast, and 36-count Edinburg.

Linen is usually stitched over two threads, although you can stitch over one to achieve even greater detail. When stitching over two threads of the linen (four squares terminology for beginners), the stitch count is half the thread count. For example, if you stitch on 28-count fabric, then 14 cross stitches would form 1" of fabric.

Plainweave fabrics other than linen that are also popular are 28-count Annabelle, 27-count Linda, 28-count Jobelan, and Lugana in counts of 20- (formerly Valerie), 25-, 28- (formerly Brittney), and 32-count.

When cutting fabric, be sure that it is 3" to 4" larger on all sides than the finished design size to allow enough space for matting and other finishing techniques.

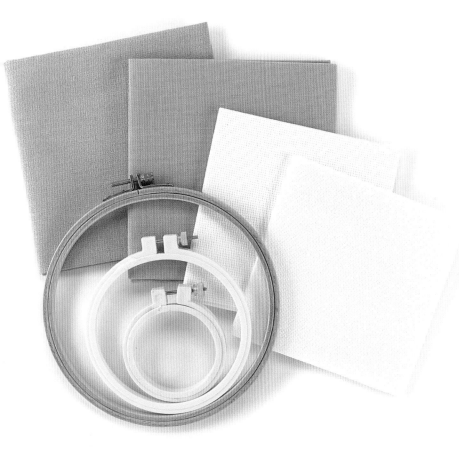

Tapestry needles come in a variety of sizes for use with the different fabric counts. See text below for a guide on which to use with each fabric.

## Needles

Cross stitch is worked with a tapestry needle that has a blunt tip and a large eye opening to accommodate more threads than a regular sewing needle.

Select a tapestry needle that is small enough not to widen the gap between the fabric threads as you stitch and one that glides easily through the fabric without piercing or splitting threads. The following is a basic guide for determining needle size. However, the combination of fabric, number of strands, and type of thread used will be the ultimate guide as to what needle size is the best to flow easily through the fabric.

For 6- and 7-count fabrics, use #20 tapestry needle.

For 8- and 10-count fabrics,

use size #22.

For 11- and 14-count, use sizes #24 through #26.

For 16- and 22-count (32-count over two threads = 16-count), use size #26.

For 18- and 36-count (over two threads = 18-count), use sizes #26 through #28.

When embellishing cross stitch with beads, attach beads using a beading needle that is finer and has a sharp point.

Never leave a needle in the design area of fabric as it will likely leave a rust stain on the fabric or even a hole in the fabric. If storing a needle on the fabric, place it on one of the outer edges that would be in the excess fabric area.

## Threads

There is a large range of threads available for cross stitching today.

Cotton embroidery floss is the most commonly used thread for counted cross stitch. This floss is 6-stranded and can be divided.

Metallic embroidery floss is a metallic thread to add glitter and sparkle to a project. It is also 6-stranded and divisible.

Rayon floss is a smooth, silky thread with a radiant shine. DMC's rayon floss is 6-stranded and Anchor's is 4-stranded. This type of floss is slippery and can be difficult to work with because it knots easily. Using shorter strands and moistening the floss with water as you stitch helps to eliminate the kinks. The extra effort in using rayon floss is

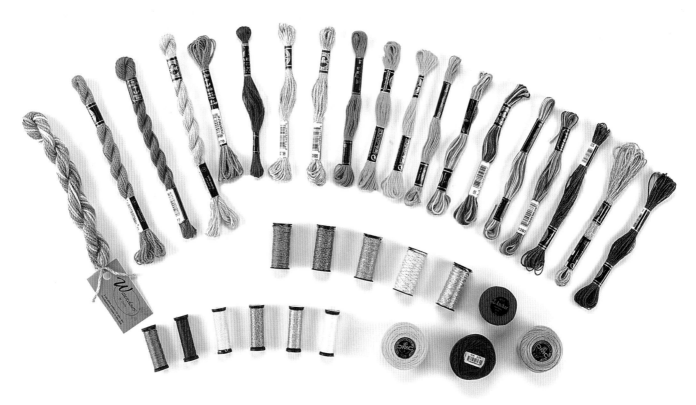

An array of threads, including cotton embroidery floss, metallic floss, rayon floss, and pearl cotton.
Thread choice depends on the overall finished look you'd like to create; however, most cross stitch is done in cotton embroidery floss.

well worth it because of its beautiful silk-like sheen.

Blending filaments and metallic threads are usually combined with other fibers to create sparkling highlights.

Pearl cotton, available in sizes 3 (thickest), 5, 8, and 12 (finest) is twisted, non-separable, and has a lustrous sheen.

Other threads include silk, wool and wool blends, Japan thread, cord, cable, silk and metallic ribbon, braid, overdyed floss, and specialty cottons such as Coton 'a Broder, flower thread, and Floche.

When working with a piece of cotton floss, cut strands 18" to avoid floss tangling. For metallics and rayons, cut strands 12" to 14" long to prevent fraying and tangling.

For best coverage, separate cotton embroidery floss strands, and then put together the number of strands required for fabric used.

Adding strands will create dimension in some designs and other designs will suggest that the number of strands be reduced to create shadows. The basic guidelines for regular counted cross stitch using cotton embroidery/metallic embroidery floss are:

For 6-, 7-, and 8-count, use six strands.

For 10- and 11-count use three to four strands.

For 14-, 16-, and 18-count use two strands.

For 28- and 32-count stitched over two threads, use two strands.

For backstitch, the usual guide is to use one strand (two at the most)—always less than the number of strands used for cross stitch.

## Determining Finished Size

To determine the size of a finished design, divide the stitch count by the number of threads per fabric inch. For example, if a design is 42 stitches wide and 84 stitches high and is stitched on a 14-count fabric, the finished size would be 3" x 6" (42 divided by 14 = 3" and 84 divided by 14 = 6").

If the same project with the same stitch count is stitched on a 28-count fabric over two threads (four squares), the finished size would still be 3" x 6". For designs stitched over two threads, divide fabric count in half and then divide into stitch count (28 divided by 2 = 14; 42 divided by 14 = 3"; and 84 divided by 14 = 6").

If the same design with the same stitch count is stitched on 28-count over one thread (square), then the finished size would be 1½" x 3", which is determined in the same manner as the first example (42 divided by 28 = 1½" and 84 divided by 28 = 3").

## Centering a Design

It is recommended that stitching start from the center point of the chart and fabric. This is the easiest method of assuring accuracy of design placement on the fabric.

To find the center of the fabric, fold the fabric in half horizontally, then vertically. Place a pin in the fold point (or pinch area with fingers) to mark the center.

Then locate the center of the design on the chart. Most charts will have arrows at top or bottom and along one side. Follow top arrow down center of chart to square lining up with side arrow.

## Charts

Each square on a chart represents a square on the fabric. Thread colors to be used per stitch (square) will have symbols assigned to them and a key code will be included with the project instructions to specify which symbol is to be used for each specific thread color. Symbols will vary among different designers and publications.

## Cleaning a Stitched Piece

When stitching is completed, wash fabric in cold water with a mild soap.

Rinse well and roll the stitched piece in a towel to remove excess water. Do not wring.

Place stitched piece right-side down on a dry towel and iron on warm setting until the stitched fabric is dry.

## Treating Stains

If a stitched piece gets a stain, don't panic. Many stains can be removed by following these few simple tips.

First apply a mild soap to the stain and soak in cold water for 15 to 30 minutes.

If a cold-water soak doesn't remove the stain, then treat the stained area with EasyWash®, rub gently, and then soak for about five minutes.

For an especially stubborn stain, the last resort is to try Orvus, which is a safe but strong horse soap. Treat the stained area as you would with the EasyWash®, but since the Orvus is stronger, use it very sparingly. Rinse well with cold water.

## Storing a Stitched Piece

Do not store a freshly washed/ironed stitched piece in a plastic bag, as mold will likely occur if the piece is not thoroughly dry. Be sure to let the stitched piece dry thoroughly for two days.

When the piece is completely dry, if possible, store it flat with white towels or white tissue separating each piece. If unable to store a stitched piece flat, then roll—not fold— the piece and store it.

Be sure to store the piece away from sunlight, as sunlight can fade the colors in the design. Also choose a dry place, as dampness can cause mildew or mold to form on the fabric.

## Basic Guidelines of Counted Cross Stitch

Wash hands before stitching. Do not put hand lotion on prior to stitching.

When stitching on Aida, an embroidery hoop helps keep the tension consistent. However, the hoop should be removed each time you stop stitching to avoid hoop marks and stubborn creases on the fabric.

If thread starts to tangle, dangle needle so that thread will untwist.

Do not knot thread, as knots can create lumps on the front of the piece when mounted; can pop through to the front on a loosely woven fabric; can lead to uneven thread tension; and can catch on the floss when stitching.

To avoid thread showing through the front, never carry thread over more than two or three squares of unstitched fabric.

Work in good light.

Never fold stitched piece. Always keep flat or roll it to avoid difficult creases.

Weave ending threads under three to four stitches. Trim excess threads.

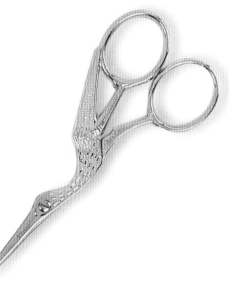

## Working with Waste Canvas

Waste canvas is used to cross stitch a design onto fabric that is not the typical, i.e. sweatshirt material. Here's how it is done:

**1.** Measure the garment front or the area to be stitched and compare the measurements to those of the charted design. Cut the waste canvas 2" to 3" larger than the design on all sides. Bind the edges of the canvas with masking tape to prevent the raw edges from snagging the garment fabric.

**2.** Center the waste canvas on the area to be stitched. The blue lines should run horizontally or vertically with the weave of the fabric to ensure that the stitched design will be straight.

**3.** Basting: To prevent the waste canvas from slipping while the design is being stitched, it is necessary to baste the waste fabric securely to the garment on all four sides, as well as diagonally, and from side to side. For larger designs, extra lines of basting may be necessary to further secure the waste canvas in place. These lines also help in centering your design.

**4.** Stitching your design: Beginning in the center, work the design in cross stitch by stitching through the canvas and the garment fabric just the way you would normally stitch on Aida fabric. Be very careful not to puncture the canvas threads. Pierced threads can be difficult to remove later. Follow the chart and color key legend of your charted design. It is suggested to use three strands for cross stitch and two for backstitch on 8.5-count

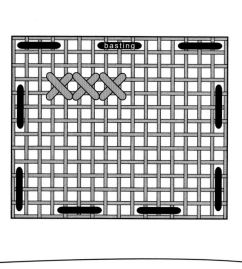

canvas, and two for cross stitch and one for backstitch on 14-count canvas.

**5.** Removing waste canvas threads: Once all stitching is complete, remove all basting stitches and trim waste canvas to within 1" of the stitched area on all sides. Dampen the waste canvas threads until they become limp. Pull out the canvas threads one at a time, using tweezers, if necessary. Be sure to pull the threads low to the fabric. Only pull in the direction of the canvas threads. Do not pull up or at an angle. Damp threads will snap or break if pulled incorrectly. To make removal of long threads easier, when working large designs, it may be helpful to cut the waste canvas threads between areas of stitching.

6. Laundering: Launder by hand only with mild liquid soap. Roll garment in a towel to remove excess water. Air dry flat. If ironing is necessary, press using a pressing cloth on the wrong side of the garment. Iron should be set on a medium heat setting.

Waste canvas instructions courtesy of Charles Craft, Inc. Charles Craft's waste fabric (canvas) is available in three count sizes: 8.5, 10, and 14.

## Stitch Diagrams

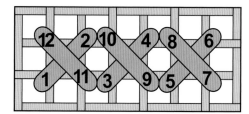

### Cross Stitch

It is important that all your stitches lay in the same direction for a better overall finish/look of your project. Bottom stitches go from the bottom left corner to the upper right corner; top stitches from bottom right corner to upper left corner. Make all the bottom stitches in a row working from left to right, then cross them as you work back from right to left.

Number 1 in the figure is the starting point of the first bottom stitch. Come up at 1, down at 2, up at 3, down at 4, up at 5, down at 6. Each stitch on the bottom row represents a half stitch.

Number 7 is the starting point of your top stitches—completing the stitches. Go up at 7, down at 8, up at 9, down at 10, up at 11, down at 12. The stitches are now full cross stitches.

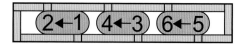

### Backstitch

Backstitch is used for outlining, lettering, and other design lines. Unless the directions state differently for a certain project, you usually backstitch with one strand (two at the most)— generally less than the number of strands used for cross stitch.

Pull the needle through at the point marked 1. Go down at 2, up at 3, down at 4, up at 5, down at 6. Continue with the forward-two-stitches, back-one-stitch pattern.

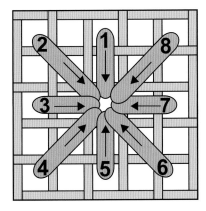

## Algerian Eye

Always stitch into the center to keep the hole clean. For a pulled stitch to create an open, lacy appearance, pull the thread as you bring the needle up. From back of fabric, come up at 1 between woven threads and go down at center. Go up at 2, down at center, up at 3, down at center, up at 5, down at center, repeating until 8 stitches are completed, leaving a small opening in the center.

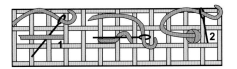

## French Knot

French knots are usually indicated by a solid dot on a chart. Use one strand of floss and bring the needle up at 1. Wrap the needle two times with the floss. Hold the floss tightly as you insert the needle back into the fabric near the same place.

At 2 on the figure, pull needle through to form a small knot on top of the fabric.

Note: In most designs where French knots are featured, you can substitute beads in place of the knots if you desire. Choose a bead color to match the floss color called for in the French knots.

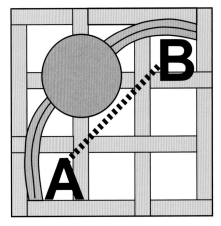

## Attaching a Bead

The easiest way to attach beads is to use a half cross stitch. From the back of fabric, come up at A. Halfway through a diagonal stitch thread the bead onto the needle, go down at B. It is recommended to stitch each bead twice to ensure that it is secure.

Beads are a popular embellishment today and with a variety of sizes and colors, you're sure to find just the right type to enhance the beauty of your stitched piece.

# Embroidery Floss Conversion Chart

This chart should be used only as a guide. It is difficult to give exact alternatives between brands since color comparisons are subject to personal preference. Conversions are given for a total of 447 solid colors in the following brands: Anchor® and DMC®.

| DMC | ANCHOR | DMC | ANCHOR | DMC | ANCHOR | DMC | ANCHOR | DMC | ANCHOR | DMC | ANCHOR |
|---|---|---|---|---|---|---|---|---|---|---|---|
| White | 2 | 422 | 943 | 721 | 925 | 869 | 944 | 3012 | 844 | 3779 | 1012 |
| Ecru | 387 | 433 | 358 | 722 | 323 | 890 | 218 | 3013 | 842 | 3781 | 904 |
| 150 | 59 | 434 | 310 | 725 | 305 | 891 | 35 | 3021 | 905 | 3782 | 899 |
| 151 | 73 | 435 | 1046 | 726 | 295 | 892 | 33 | 3022 | 8581 | 3787 | 273 |
| 152 | 969 | 436 | 1045 | 727 | 293 | 893 | 28 | 3023 | 1040 | 3790 | 393 |
| 153 | 95 | 437 | 362 | 728 | 305 | 894 | 27 | 3024 | 397 | 3799 | 236 |
| 154 | 873 | 444 | 290 | 729 | 890 | 895 | 1044 | 3031 | 905 | 3801 | 1098 |
| 155 | 1030 | 445 | 288 | 730 | 845 | 898 | 360 | 3032 | 903 | 3802 | 1019 |
| 156 | 118 | 451 | 233 | 732 | 281 | 899 | 52 | 3033 | 391 | 3803 | 972 |
| 157 | 120 | 452 | 676 | 733 | 280 | 900 | 333 | 3041 | 871 | 3804 | 63 |
| 158 | 178 | 453 | 231 | 734 | 279 | 902 | 897 | 3042 | 870 | 3805 | 62 |
| 159 | 120 | 469 | 267 | 738 | 372 | 904 | 258 | 3045 | 888 | 3806 | 62 |
| 160 | 175 | 470 | 267 | 739 | 387 | 905 | 257 | 3046 | 945 | 3807 | 122 |
| 161 | 176 | 471 | 266 | 740 | 316 | 906 | 256 | 3047 | 852 | 3808 | 1068 |
| 162 | 159 | 472 | 253 | 741 | 304 | 907 | 255 | 3051 | 681 | 3809 | 1066 |
| 163 | 877 | 498 | 1005 | 742 | 303 | 909 | 923 | 3052 | 262 | 3810 | 1066 |
| 164 | 240 | 500 | 683 | 743 | 302 | 910 | 229 | 3053 | 261 | 3811 | 1060 |
| 165 | 278 | 501 | 878 | 744 | 301 | 911 | 205 | 3064 | 883 | 3812 | 188 |
| 166 | 280 | 502 | 877 | 745 | 300 | 912 | 209 | 3072 | 847 | 3813 | 875 |
| 167 | 374 | 503 | 876 | 746 | 275 | 913 | 204 | 3078 | 292 | 3814 | 1074 |
| 168 | 234 | 505 | 210 | 747 | 158 | 915 | 1029 | 3325 | 129 | 3815 | 877 |
| 169 | 235 | 517 | 162 | 754 | 1012 | 917 | 89 | 3326 | 36 | 3816 | 876 |
| 208 | 110 | 518 | 1039 | 758 | 9575 | 918 | 341 | 3328 | 1024 | 3817 | 875 |
| 209 | 109 | 519 | 1038 | 760 | 1022 | 919 | 340 | 3340 | 329 | 3818 | 923 |
| 210 | 108 | 520 | 862 | 761 | 1021 | 920 | 1004 | 3341 | 328 | 3819 | 278 |
| 211 | 342 | 522 | 860 | 762 | 234 | 921 | 1003 | 3345 | 268 | 3820 | 306 |
| 221 | 897 | 523 | 859 | 772 | 259 | 922 | 1003 | 3346 | 267 | 3821 | 305 |
| 223 | 895 | 524 | 858 | 775 | 128 | 924 | 840 | 3347 | 266 | 3822 | 295 |
| 224 | 893 | 535 | 401 | 777 | 65 | 926 | 838 | 3348 | 264 | 3823 | 386 |
| 225 | 1026 | 543 | 933 | 778 | 968 | 927 | 837 | 3350 | 59 | 3824 | 8 |
| 300 | 352 | 550 | 102 | 779 | 380 | 928 | 847 | 3354 | 74 | 3825 | 323 |
| 301 | 1049 | 552 | 99 | 780 | 309 | 930 | 1035 | 3362 | 263 | 3826 | 1049 |
| 304 | 1006 | 553 | 98 | 782 | 308 | 931 | 1034 | 3363 | 262 | 3827 | 311 |
| 307 | 289 | 554 | 96 | 783 | 307 | 932 | 1033 | 3364 | 260 | 3828 | 373 |
| 309 | 42 | 561 | 212 | 791 | 178 | 934 | 862 | 3371 | 382 | 3829 | 901 |
| 310 | 403 | 562 | 210 | 792 | 941 | 935 | 269 | 3607 | 87 | 3830 | 5975 |
| 311 | 148 | 563 | 208 | 793 | 176 | 936 | 269 | 3608 | 86 | 3831 | 29 |
| 312 | 979 | 564 | 206 | 794 | 175 | 937 | 268 | 3609 | 85 | 3832 | 28 |
| 315 | 1019 | 580 | 281 | 796 | 133 | 938 | 381 | 3685 | 1028 | 3833 | 26 |
| 316 | 1017 | 581 | 280 | 797 | 132 | 939 | 152 | 3687 | 68 | 3834 | 100 |
| 317 | 400 | 597 | 1064 | 798 | 131 | 943 | 188 | 3688 | 66 | 3835 | 98 |
| 318 | 399 | 598 | 1062 | 799 | 136 | 945 | 881 | 3689 | 49 | 3836 | 90 |
| 319 | 218 | 600 | 59 | 800 | 144 | 946 | 332 | 3705 | 35 | 3837 | 100 |
| 320 | 215 | 601 | 57 | 801 | 359 | 947 | 330 | 3706 | 33 | 3838 | 177 |
| 321 | 9046 | 602 | 63 | 803 | 149 | 948 | 1011 | 3708 | 31 | 3839 | 176 |
| 322 | 978 | 603 | 62 | 807 | 168 | 950 | 4146 | 3712 | 1023 | 3840 | 117 |
| 326 | 59 | 604 | 55 | 809 | 130 | 951 | 1010 | 3713 | 1020 | 3841 | 9159 |
| 327 | 100 | 605 | 1094 | 813 | 161 | 954 | 203 | 3716 | 25 | 3842 | 164 |
| 333 | 119 | 606 | 334 | 814 | 45 | 955 | 206 | 3721 | 896 | 3843 | 1089 |
| 334 | 977 | 608 | 332 | 815 | 44 | 956 | 41 | 3722 | 1027 | 3844 | 410 |
| 335 | 38 | 610 | 889 | 816 | 1005 | 957 | 50 | 3726 | 1018 | 3845 | 1089 |
| 336 | 150 | 611 | 898 | 817 | 13 | 958 | 187 | 3727 | 1016 | 3846 | 1090 |
| 340 | 118 | 612 | 832 | 818 | 23 | 959 | 186 | 3731 | 76 | 3847 | 1076 |
| 341 | 117 | 613 | 831 | 819 | 271 | 961 | 76 | 3733 | 75 | 3848 | 1074 |
| 347 | 1025 | 632 | 936 | 820 | 134 | 962 | 75 | 3740 | 872 | 3849 | 1070 |
| 349 | 13 | 640 | 903 | 822 | 390 | 963 | 73 | 3743 | 869 | 3850 | 189 |
| 350 | 11 | 642 | 392 | 823 | 152 | 964 | 185 | 3746 | 1030 | 3851 | 187 |
| 351 | 10 | 644 | 830 | 824 | 164 | 966 | 206 | 3747 | 120 | 3852 | 306 |
| 352 | 9 | 645 | 273 | 825 | 162 | 967 | 6 | 3750 | 1036 | 3853 | 1003 |
| 353 | 6 | 646 | 8581 | 826 | 161 | 970 | 316 | 3752 | 1032 | 3854 | 313 |
| 355 | 1014 | 647 | 1040 | 827 | 160 | 972 | 298 | 3753 | 1031 | 3855 | 311 |
| 356 | 5975 | 648 | 900 | 828 | 9159 | 973 | 297 | 3755 | 140 | 3856 | 1010 |
| 367 | 217 | 666 | 46 | 829 | 906 | 975 | 355 | 3756 | 1037 | 3857 | 936 |
| 368 | 214 | 676 | 891 | 830 | 277 | 976 | 1001 | 3760 | 169 | 3858 | 1007 |
| 369 | 1043 | 677 | 956 | 831 | 277 | 977 | 1002 | 3761 | 928 | 3859 | 914 |
| 370 | 855 | 680 | 901 | 832 | 907 | 986 | 246 | 3765 | 170 | 3860 | 678 |
| 371 | 854 | 699 | 923 | 833 | 907 | 987 | 244 | 3766 | 167 | 3861 | 677 |
| 372 | 853 | 700 | 228 | 834 | 874 | 988 | 243 | 3768 | 779 | 3862 | 358 |
| 400 | 351 | 701 | 227 | 837 | 927 | 989 | 242 | 3770 | 1009 | 3863 | 379 |
| 402 | 1047 | 702 | 226 | 838 | 1088 | 991 | 1076 | 3771 | 336 | 3864 | 376 |
| 407 | 914 | 703 | 238 | 839 | 1086 | 992 | 1072 | 3772 | 1007 | 3865 | 2 |
| 413 | 236 | 704 | 256 | 840 | 1084 | 993 | 1070 | 3774 | 778 | 3866 | 926 |
| 414 | 235 | 712 | 926 | 841 | 1082 | 995 | 410 | 3776 | 1048 | B5200 | 1 |
| 415 | 398 | 718 | 88 | 842 | 1080 | 996 | 433 | 3777 | 1015 | | |
| 420 | 375 | 720 | 326 | 844 | 1041 | 3011 | 846 | 3778 | 1013 | | |

# Gifts for
# Anniversaries

# 50th Wedding Anniversary Album

**Design by Roberta Madeleine**

*A golden anniversary calls for an elaborate celebration. The 50th Wedding Anniversary Album Cover is a gold/cream Lugana fabric trimmed with Cluny lace that can fit any standard-size three-ring binder with a 1½" spine. The embellishment of gold fibers and pearl beads give a richness and elegance fitting for the commemoration of this marriage milestone. The album will help the couple cherish their golden years with pictures from years past.*

**Cross Stitch:** 2 strands
**Backstitch:** 2 strands
**Stitch Count:** 66 wide x 84 high
**Approximate Finished Size:**
 20-count fabric <u>stitched over two threads</u> = 10-count
10-count fabric: 6½" wide x 8¾" high

**Supplies**
- Beautiful Accents™ 20-Count Gold/Cream Lugana Prefinished Album Cover
- DMC® 6-Strand Embroidery Floss (1 skein each color)
- 1 package Mill Hill #02001 Pearl Seed Beads
- 1 spool Kreinik™ Fine Braid #002, Gold
- DMC® Metallic Floss (1 skein each color)
- #22 Tapestry Needle
- Beading Needle
- Photo Album, Scrapbook, or Standard Three-Ring Binder (optional)

## General Instructions

This project must be **stitched over two threads** on the 20-count Lugana in order for it to fit within the prefinished album cover.

The beads are stitched with white floss inside each border diagonal.

### DMC® 6-Strand Embroidery Floss
| | | |
|---|---|---|
| ◣ | 834 | Golden Olive, very light |
| ✚ | 3822 | Straw, light |
| △ | 3823 | Yellow, ultra pale |
| – | White | White |

### DMC® 6-Strand Metallic Floss
| | | |
|---|---|---|
| ♡ | 5282 | Gold, light |
| ○ | 5283 | Gold, dark |

### Kreinik™ Fine Braid
| | | |
|---|---|---|
| ■ | 002 | Gold |

## Backstitch Instructions
Buds, stems, and words: DMC 831 Golden Olive, medium.
Names and date: DMC 830 Golden Olive, dark.
Border: Kreinik Fine Braid 002 Gold.
Cross-hatched lines on "50": Kreinik Fine Braid 002 Gold.

## Bead Instructions
- Stitch pearl seed beads with white floss. Refer to "Attaching a Bead" section in General Instructions, page 11, for further assistance, if necessary.

# Anniversary Frames

### Design by Ursula Michael

*Frames are popular anniversary gifts. This acrylic frame comes with a pre-cut vinyl weave for stitching. Numbers are provided for personalizing with the couple's anniversary year. For a silver anniversary, stitch "25" in silver metallic. When cross stitch is completed, place the stitched vinyl weave and couple's picture into the frame for a personal keepsake to carry them through even more happy years together.*

**Cross Stitch:** 2 strands
**Stitch Count:** 73 wide x 91 high
**Approximate Finished Size:**
   18-count fabric: 4" wide x 5" high

**Supplies**
- Crafter's Pride Easel-Back Acrylic Frame with Crafter's Pride 18-Count White Vinyl Weave
- DMC® 6-Strand Embroidery Floss (1 skein each color)
- #26 Tapestry Needle

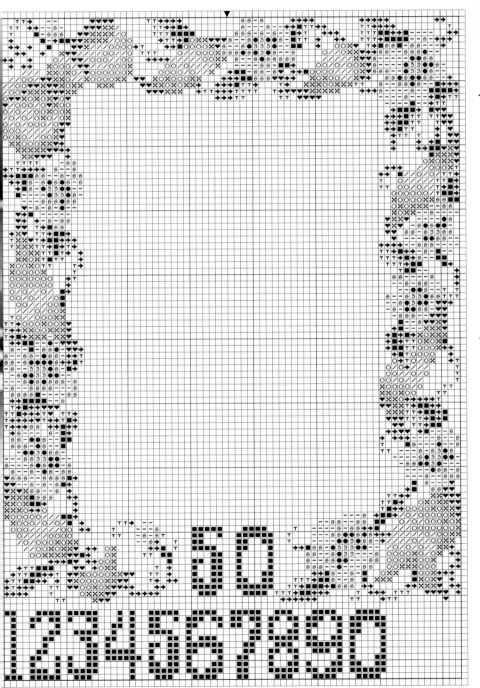

### DMC® 6-Strand Embroidery Floss

| Symbol | No. | Color |
|---|---|---|
| ● | 347 | Salmon, very dark |
| 3 | 726 | Topaz, light |
| 5 | 760 | Salmon |
| ♥ | 796 | Royal Blue, dark |
| ✕ | 798 | Delft Blue, dark |
| / | 800 | Delft Blue, pale |
| ○ | 809 | Delft Blue |
| ■ | 895 | Hunter Green, very dark |
| ➜ | 3347 | Yellow Green, medium |
| T | 3348 | Yellow Green, light |
| — | 3713 | Salmon, very light |

"50": DMC gold metallic floss
"25": DMC silver metallic floss

# Gifts for
# Babies

# Panda Baby Bear Album, Bib, and Towel Set

### Designs by Pam Kellogg

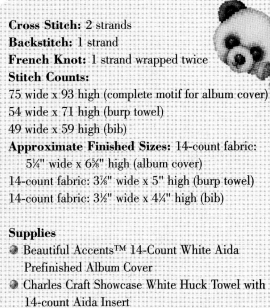

*This precious panda baby will be the star of the baby shower—and with the expectant parents! The baby album, for all those keepsake pictures, is pre-finished so there's no sewing except for cross stitch. And the cute companion pieces include a coordinating burp towel and baby bib, both of which serve important roles in baby's first year.*

**Cross Stitch:** 2 strands
**Backstitch:** 1 strand
**French Knot:** 1 strand wrapped twice
**Stitch Counts:**
75 wide x 93 high (complete motif for album cover)
54 wide x 71 high (burp towel)
49 wide x 59 high (bib)
**Approximate Finished Sizes:** 14-count fabric:
   5¼" wide x 6⅝" high (album cover)
14-count fabric: 3⅞" wide x 5" high (burp towel)
14-count fabric: 3½" wide x 4¼" high (bib)

**Supplies**
- Beautiful Accents™ 14-Count White Aida Prefinished Album Cover
- Charles Craft Showcase White Huck Towel with 14-count Aida Insert
- Zweigart® 14-count White Aida Baby Bib #BG3706/001
- DMC® 6-Strand Embroidery Floss (2 skeins each color for complete set)
- #24 Tapestry Needle

## Album Cover

Stitch complete motif centered on album cover.

## Burp Towel

Omitting outer border, stitch remaining motif centered on towel.

## Pink Bow Bib

Stitch only bear, bow, and "Baby" centered on bib.

## Green Bow Bib

To change pink bow color to sea green colors, make the following substitutions:

- 3847 instead of 309
- 3348 instead of 335
- 958 instead of 776
- 964 instead of 818
- 3812 instead of 899
- 959 instead of 3326
- Backstitch in 3847

## Backstitch Instructions

Ears, eyes, nose, and mouth: DMC 310 Black.
Bear muzzle: DMC 317 Pewter Gray.
Bow: DMC 326 Rose, very dark.
Curlicues: DMC 964 Sea Green, light.
"Baby": DMC 3812 Sea Green, very dark.

---

### DMC® 6-Strand Embroidery Floss

| | | |
|---|---|---|
| ♡ | 309 | Rose, deep |
| ■ | 310 | Black |
| ↘ | 317 | Pewter Gray |
| $ | 318 | Steel Gray, light |
| ◢ | 335 | Rose |
| ♥ | 413 | Pewter Gray, dark |
| ✖ | 414 | Steel Gray, dark |
| ★ | 415 | Pearl Gray |
| + | 745 | Yellow, light pale |
| 4 | 762 | Pearl Gray, very light |
| m | 776 | Pink, medium |
| ➔ | 818 | Baby Pink |
| 3 | 899 | Rose, medium |
| ꙍ | 958 | Sea Green, dark |
| ◕ | 959 | Sea Green, medium |
| Z | 964 | Sea Green, light |
| ✗ | 3326 | Rose, light |
| 2 | 3799 | Pewter Gray, very dark |
| ♠ | 3812 | Sea Green, very dark |
| · | White | White |

---

## French Knot Instructions

● Eyes and nose: DMC White.

# Baby Frame

**Design by Ursula Michael**

*Colorful motifs adorn this attractive baby frame that's suitable for boys and girls.
The acrylic frame comes with a pre-cut vinyl weave for stitching. When cross stitch is
completed, place stitched vinyl weave and baby's picture into frame.*

*Take a weekend to make this precious frame that will be enjoyed for generations!*

## DMC® 6-Strand Embroidery Floss

| | | |
|---|---|---|
| m | 210 | Lavender, medium |
| ■ | 676 | Old Gold, light |
| ♥ | 726 | Topaz, light |
| ✖ | 799 | Delft Blue, medium |
| ★ | 800 | Delft Blue, pale |
| 3 | 913 | Nile Green, medium |
| 2 | 962 | Dusty Rose, medium |

## Backstitch Instructions

Star and rabbit pin: DMC 799 Delft Blue, medium.
Broken line around the center of frame: DMC 962 Dusty Rose, medium.

**Cross Stitch:** 2 strands
**Backstitch:** 1 strand
**Stitch Count:** 74 wide x 91 high
**Approximate Finished Size:**
   18-count fabric: 4" wide x 5" high

**Supplies**
● Crafter's Pride Easel-Back Acrylic Frame
   with Crafter's Pride 18-Count White
   Vinyl Weave
● DMC® 6-Strand Embroidery Floss
   (1 skein each color)
● #26 Tapestry Needle

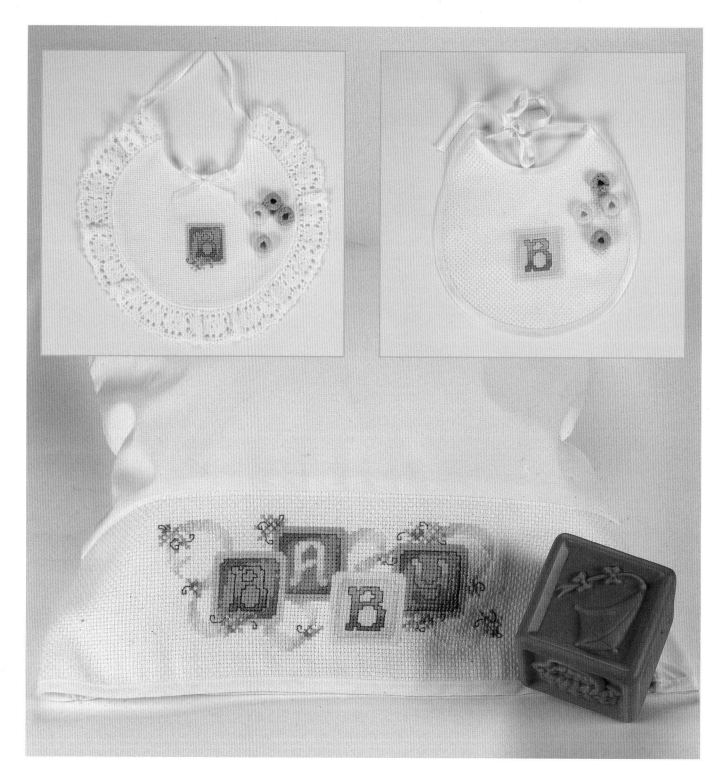

# Baby Blocks Pillowcase and Bib

### *Design by Pam Kellogg*

*Oh baby! Baby has his or her own special pillowcase. The prefinished baby pillowcase with an Aida section is great for boys and girls. All you need to do to complete this pretty pillowcase is cross stitch the colorful theme of baby blocks. As a companion gift to the pillowcase, stitch one of the "B" motifs on a prefinished baby bib. There's a lacy bib for the girls and a bib with a binding trim for boys.*

## Girl Bib

Stitch pink "B" block motif with flowers on 14-count bib.

## Boy Bib

Stitch yellow "B" block motif on 10-count bib.

### DMC® 6-Strand Embroidery Floss

| | | |
|---|---|---|
| 3 | 518 | Wedgewood, light |
| ⌐ | 519 | Sky Blue |
| ★ | 725 | Topaz |
| 4 | 726 | Topaz, light |
| ⊥ | 727 | Topaz, very light |
| 2 | 958 | Sea Green, dark |
| ♥ | 959 | Sea Green, medium |
| ♡ | 962 | Dusty Rose, medium |
| z | 963 | Dusty Rose, ultra very light |
| ⊘ | 964 | Sea Green, light |
| // | 3078 | Golden Yellow, very light |
| ◨ | 3716 | Dusty Rose, very light |
| m | 3761 | Sky Blue, light |

### Backstitch Instructions

"A" and inside the yellow block: DMC 725 Topaz.
"Y" and inside the pink block: DMC 961 Dusty Rose, dark.
Blue "B" and inside the blue block: DMC 3760 Wedgewood.
Green "B," inside the green block, and the curlicues:
DMC 3812 Sea Green, very dark.

**Cross Stitch:** 2 strands
**Backstitch:** 1 strand
**Stitch Counts:** 94 wide x 37 high (pillowcase)
  20 wide x 23 high ("B" motif for girl bib)
  20 wide x 20 high ("B" motif for boy bib)
**Approximate Finished Sizes:**
  14-count fabric:
  6⅝" wide x 2⅝" high (pillowcase)
  14-count fabric: 1½" wide x 1⅝" high
  ("B" block with flowers for girl bib)
  10-count fabric: 1½" wide x 1½" high
  ("B" block with for boy bib)

### Supplies

- Beautiful Accents™ 14-Count White Prefinished Baby Pillowcase
- DMC® 6-Strand Embroidery Floss (1 skein each color)
- Beautiful Accents™ 14-Count White Prefinished Lacy Baby Bib
- 10-Count White Damask Prefinished Baby Bib
- #24 Tapestry Needle

**Cross Stitch:** 2 strands
**Backstitch:** 1 strand, except for smiles and
   birds' beaks, which require 2 strands
**French Knot:** 1 strand wrapped twice
**Stitch Count:**
   147 wide x 36 high (complete towel motif)
   56 wide x 28 high (mitt motif)
**Approximate Finished Sizes:**
   16-count fabric: 9¼" wide x 2¼" high (towel)
   16-count fabric: 3½" wide x 1¾" high (mitt)

**Supplies**
● Zweigart® Terrycloth Hooded Bath Towel
   and Mitt Set with 16-Count Aida Inserts
   (white with blue trim)
● Anchor® 6-Strand Embroidery Floss
   (1 skein each color)
● #26 Tapestry Needle

# Whale of a Bath Time Hooded Bath Towel and Bath Mitt

**Design by Jane Blum**

   Splish, splash, the baby's having a whale of
a time in the bath! Any baby will love the feel of
this luxuriously soft terry bath towel and mitt.
The theme of bathing whales is appropriate for
boys and girls.

## Anchor® 6-Strand Embroidery Floss

| | | |
|---|---|---|
| ☆ | 1 | Snow White |
| m | 50 | China Rose, medium |
| ◖ | 52 | China Rose, medium dark |
| ▼ | 108 | Lavender, very light |
| ★ | 109 | Lavender, light |
| ✖ | 130 | Cobalt Blue, medium light |
| 3 | 136 | Wedgwood, light |
| ✪ | 144 | Delft Blue, very light |
| ✕ | 206 | Spruce, light |
| ♡ | 208 | Spruce, medium light |
| ↶ | 254 | Parrot Green, light |
| 2 | 295 | Jonquil, medium light |
| ♥ | 297 | Jonquil, medium |
| ◩ | 399 | Gray, medium light |
| ⊘ | 400 | Gray, medium |
| ■ | 403 | Black |
| Z | 1030 | Thistle, medium dark |

## General Instructions

Stitch complete motif on the hooded bath towel.

For the mitt, stitch only the beginning of the motif (in front of whale) containing the large fish and two small fish, along with the one bird that is closest to the fish. For additional reference, see photograph.

## Backstitch Instructions

Smiles: two strands Anchor 52 China Rose, medium dark.

Waterspout and splash lines: one strand Anchor 130 Cobalt Blue, medium light.

Birds' beaks: two strands Anchor 295 Jonquil, medium light.

Sun: one strand Anchor 297 Jonquil, medium.

Whale, whale's eye, and the fish: one strand Anchor 403 Black.

## French Knot Instructions

• Eyes: one strand Anchor 403 Black wrapped twice.

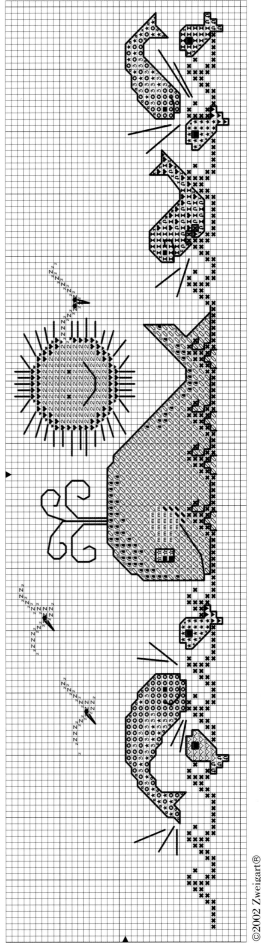

# Gifts for Birthdays

# Birthday Bear

### Design by Phyllis Dobbs

*Bears have always been a favorite with children… and many adults, too. DMC's birthday bear is a great personalized memento of a birthday. And best of all, the banner only takes an hour to stitch!*

## General Instructions

The birthday bear comes with a solid red Aida banner; however, the project shown was stitched on a 16-count stitchband. The 16-count provided more design space.

Center stitching on the stitchband to go across the bear as a banner. When stitching is completed, baste the stitchband ends together. The ends will be at the center of the bear's back.

**Cross Stitch:** 2 strands
**Backstitch:** 2 strands
**Stitch Count:**
  34 wide x 11 high
**Approximate Finished**
  **Size:** 16-count fabric:
  2⅛" wide x ¾" high
**Supplies**
- DMC® Birthday Bear
- Zweigart® 16-Count White Stitchband with Red Trim #7003/019
- DMC® 6-Strand Embroidery Floss (1 skein each color)
- #26 Tapestry Needle

## DMC® 6-Strand Embroidery Floss

| | | |
|---|---|---|
| ● | 321 | Christmas Red |
| ♡ | 726 | Topaz, light |
| □ | 798 | Delft Blue, dark |
| ▼ | 911 | Emerald Green, medium |

## Backstitch Instructions

Balloon strings and "Happy Birthday": DMC 796 Royal Blue, dark.

Name: DMC 911 Emerald Green, medium.

©2002 The DMC Corporation

# Birthday
# Table Topper

### Design by Phyllis Dobbs

*I love celebrating birthdays. For me, it's celebrating life…and life is precious.*

*Make every birthday party even more special with this festive birthday table topper. The 10-count prefinished table topper makes stitching quick and easy. The primary colors are great for any age—adults and children. Stitch this birthday table topper in one weekend to celebrate birthdays for years to come.*

**Cross Stitch:** 3 strands
**Backstitch:** 2 strands (balloons)
**Long Stitch:** 1 strand (balloon strings)
**Stitch Count:**
    47 wide x 45 high (balloon/bow motif)
    108 wide x 48 high ("Happy Birthday")
**Approximate Finished Size:**
    10-count fabric: 4¾" wide x 4½" high (balloon/bow motif)
    10-count fabric: 10⅞" wide x 4⅞" high ("Happy Birthday" motif)
**Supplies**
- Zweigart® 10-Count White Damask Largo Prefinished Table Topper
- DMC® 6-Strand Embroidery Floss (2 skeins each color)
- #22 Tapestry Needle

*Happy Birthday*

## General Instructions

Stitch "Happy Birthday" centered in the Aida strip of the table topper.

Stitch balloon/bow motif on each side of "Happy Birthday" at the ends of the topper.

Turn table topper and repeat designs on opposite side.

### DMC® 6-Strand Embroidery Floss

| | | |
|---|---|---|
| ▲ | 321 | Christmas Red |
| ✕ | 726 | Topaz, light |
| ✚ | 798 | Delft Blue, dark |
| ● | 911 | Emerald Green, medium |
| ○ | White | White |

## Backstitch Instructions
Balloons: DMC 310 Black.

## Long Stitch Instructions
Balloon strings: DMC 797 Royal Blue.

# Gifts for Christmas

# Christmas Tree Jar Lacy

*Design by Pam Kellogg*

*Jar lacies are popular because they are inexpensive, quick-to-stitch gifts. Fill a large Mason®-type jar with homemade goodies such as fudge, cookies, spiced tea, candy, or potpourri. Then place a festive jar lacy on top. It's good to have a supply of jar lacies on hand for last-minute gifts.*

## DMC® 6-Strand Embroidery Floss

| | | |
|---|---|---|
| ■ | 561 | Jade, very dark |
| m | 562 | Jade, medium |
| ♥ | 563 | Jade, light |
| 2 | 564 | Jade, very light |
| ◣ | 955 | Nile Green, light |

## Kreinik™ #4 Braid

| | | |
|---|---|---|
| ♡ | 002 | Gold |
| ✖ | 029 | Turquoise |
| ★ | 031 | Crimson |

## Backstitch Instructions

Garland and star: Kreinik #002 Gold.

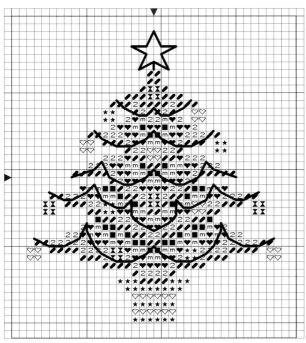

**Cross Stitch:** 2 strands (floss); 1 strand (braid)
**Backstitch:** 1 strand (floss); 1 strand (braid)
**Stitch Count:** 34 wide x 38 high
**Approximate Finished Size:**
 18-count fabric: 1⅞" wide x 2" high

### Supplies
- Beautiful Accents™ 18-Count White Prefinished Large Jar Lacy with White Ribbon
- DMC® 6-Strand Embroidery Floss (1 skein each color)
- Jar (large mouth)
- Kreinik™ #4 Braid (1 spool each color)
- #26 Tapestry Needle

©2002 X-Stitch Enterprises

**Cross Stitch:** 1 strand (#3 pearl cotton)
**Backstitch:** 1 strand (#3 pearl cotton)
**Stitch Counts:** 61 wide x 61 high (skating motif)
   62 wide x 61 high shoveling snow motif)
   63 wide x 54 high ('Tis the Season motif)
**Approximate Finished Size:**
   18-count fabric <u>stitched over two threads</u> = 9-count
   9-count fabric: 6¾" wide x 6¾" high
   (approximate for all three designs)
**Supplies**
- 6 Zweigart® 18-count Blue-and-White Tannenbaum
  Fabric Squares (three squares are used as backing fabric
  for the pillows)
- DMC® #3 Pearl Cotton
  (2 skeins of each color for all three designs)
- 3 Square Pillow Forms 12" or 1 bag Polyfil
- #24 Tapestry Needle
- Sewing Machine and White Thread

# Frosty Folks Pillows

***Designs by Ursula Michael***

*'Tis the season for a white
Christmas…inside the house! Blue
and white Tannebaum is the perfect
background fabric for the playful
Frosty Folks. Nestled among snowflake
and tree motifs, Frosty Folks enjoy the
holiday season.*

*A coordinating afghan would
complete the wintertime setting—
along with a cup of hot chocolate.*

## General Instructions

These designs were stitched over two threads on 18-count Tannenbaum fabric squares.

## Floss Instructions

If stitching with 6-strand embroidery floss in place of the #3 pearl cotton, use three strands of floss for cross stitch and two strands for backstitch. The color numbers would be the same for the embroidery floss as shown for the pearl cotton.

## Pillow Instructions

When cross stitch is complete, place finished square right sides together with one of the unfinished fabric squares. Pin to hold in place and machine stitch with ¼" seam allowance around the perimeter of the pillow, leaving a 2" opening for turning and stuffing.

Turn pillow right-side out, insert pillow form or Polyfil, and hand-stitch turn-hole closed.

## Afghan Instructions

Afghan fabric should contain three squares across and four squares down.

Starting with top left corner of afghan, stitch the shoveling snow motif, skip a square, and stitch the skating motif in the top right corner.

For the second row, skip the first square, stitch 'Tis the Season motif in the center square, skip the third square.

On the third row, stitch the skating motif in the first square, skip the second square, and stitch the shoveling motif in the third square.

For the fourth row, skip the first square, stitch 'Tis the Season motif in the center square, and leave the last square blank. Fringe.

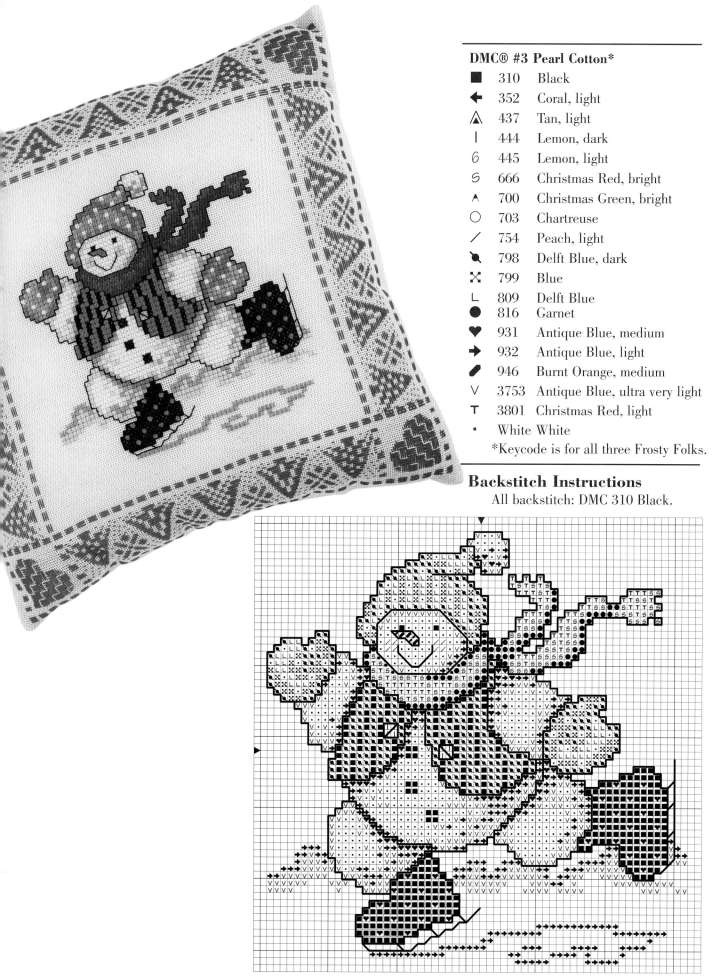

**DMC® #3 Pearl Cotton***

| | | |
|---|---|---|
| ■ | 310 | Black |
| ← | 352 | Coral, light |
| △ | 437 | Tan, light |
| I | 444 | Lemon, dark |
| 6 | 445 | Lemon, light |
| 5 | 666 | Christmas Red, bright |
| Λ | 700 | Christmas Green, bright |
| O | 703 | Chartreuse |
| / | 754 | Peach, light |
| ✎ | 798 | Delft Blue, dark |
| X | 799 | Blue |
| L | 809 | Delft Blue |
| ● | 816 | Garnet |
| ♥ | 931 | Antique Blue, medium |
| → | 932 | Antique Blue, light |
| ◢ | 946 | Burnt Orange, medium |
| V | 3753 | Antique Blue, ultra very light |
| T | 3801 | Christmas Red, light |
| · | White | White |

*Keycode is for all three Frosty Folks.

## Backstitch Instructions

All backstitch: DMC 310 Black.

# Whimsical Santa Tree Skirt and Ornaments

### Designs by Ursula Michael

*You're sure to catch the spirit of the holiday season with these Whimsical Santas. They skate around decorated trees on a snow-white tree skirt and then the same festive fellows are featured as tree ornaments.*

*Notice the two different looks. The Santas and trees on the 14-count tree skirt were stitched over two threads, thereby equaling 7-count fabric. The Santa ornaments were stitched on 18-count vinyl weave.*

*These Whimsical Santa Tree Skirt and Ornaments will bring joy for many Christmases to come!*

**Cross Stitch:** 1 strand (#3 pearl cotton for tree skirt)
2 strands (embroidery floss for ornaments)
**Backstitch:** 1 strand (#3 pearl cotton for tree skirt)
1 strand (embroidery floss for ornaments)
**Stitch Counts:** 55 wide x 51 high (Santa #1)
57 wide x 58 high (Santa #2)
50 wide x 56 high (Santa #3)
42 wide x 54 high (Tree)
**Approximate Finished Sizes:**
14-count fabric stitched over two threads = 7-count
7-count fabric: 8" wide x 8" high (each Santa)
7-count fabric: 7" wide x 9" high (each Tree)
18-count fabric: 3" wide x 3" high (each Santa)

**Supplies**
- Beautiful Accents ™ 14-Count White Aida Prefinished Tree Skirt
- Anchor® #3 Pearl Cotton
  - 1 skein each #9, #290, #367, #370, #392, and #398
  - 2 skeins each #46 and #1012
  - 3 skeins #403
  - 5 skeins white
  - 6 skeins each #20 and #245
- Crafter's Pride 18-Count White Vinyl Weave
- Anchor® 6-Strand Embroidery Floss
  - 1 skein each of the colors in keycode
- 3 Pieces 5" Square Red Felt
- 3 5"-Long Strips Red Chenille Ribbon
- #22 Tapestry Needle (tree skirt)
- #26 Tapestry Needle (ornaments)
- Fabric Glue
- Scissors

## Tree Skirt

Measure 8" from the center top of the tree skirt. Santa #2 should be in this location, leaving 2" from the bottom of the Santa motif and the beginning of the lace trim.

Santa #1 (on left of Santa #2) and Santa #3 (on the right of Santa #2) have a tree between them and Santa #2. When stitching the trees, measure down 7½" from the top of the tree skirt, again leaving a 2" space between the bottom of the tree motif and the beginning of the lace trim. Position the tree trunk to be facing straight down to the lace trim.

To reconfirm the design's position, measure 2" from the beginning of the lace trim. Then count the rows upwards of the design. For the Santa motifs, you should have approximately 8" from the top and for the tree, 7½". It's important for the bottom row of Santas and trees to all be 2" from the beginning of the lace trim. This will give the finished skirt continuity overall.

Pearl cotton #3 was used for stitching the tree skirt over two threads.

## Ornaments

Stitch Santas on 18-count vinyl weave.

When stitching is complete, use scissors to trim excess fabric around the stitched area.

Glue the back of the work to a square of red felt. Fold the chenille ribbon in half and insert between the felt and stitched work. Let dry.

Trim felt around the vinyl weave.

Six-strand embroidery floss was used for stitching the ornaments. One skein of each color was used.

## Backstitch Instructions

All backstitch: Anchor 403 Black.

### Anchor® #3 Pearl Cotton (for tree skirt)

| | | |
|---|---|---|
| · | White | White |
| ♥ | 9 | Coral, light |
| ✖ | 20 | Garnet |
| ♡ | 46 | Christmas Red, bright |
| ▲ | 245 | Christmas Green, bright |
| + | 290 | Lemon, dark |
| ◊ | 367 | Tan, very light |
| ↆ | 370 | Brown, light |
| ★ | 392 | Beige Gray, dark |
| ⁞ | 398 | Pearl Gray |
| ■ | 403 | Black |
| T | 1012 | Peach, light |

Note: The color numbers would be the same for stitching ornaments with 6-strand embroidery floss.

Santa #1

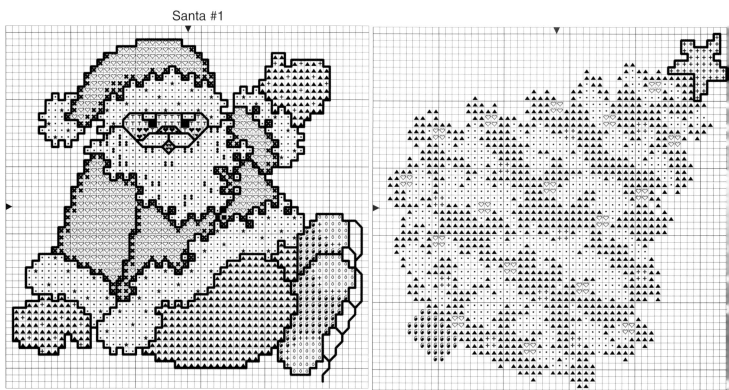

©2002 Anchor®

Santa #2

Santa #3

# Gifts for Father's Day

# Dad Bookmark

### Design by Ursula Michael

*Show dad he's a special star in your book with this handmade bookmark. Stitched on a stitchband, this is a quick-to-stitch and an inexpensive gift, yet it's a gift any father is sure to treasure.*

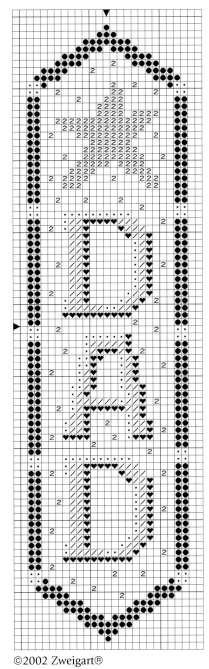

## General Instructions

Center design on stitchband and stitch.

When cross stitch is completed, press stitchband. Trim excess fabric at both ends of bookmark.

Finish bookmark by folding ¼" at each end and slipstitching on the back of bookmark.

### Anchor® 6-Strand Embroidery Floss

| | | |
|---|---|---|
| • | 2 | White |
| ● | 46 | Crimson Red |
| / | 128 | Cobalt Blue, light |
| ♥ | 148 | Delft Blue, medium |

### Kreinik™ #4 Braid

| | | |
|---|---|---|
| 2 | 002 | Gold |

**Cross Stitch:** 2 strands
**Stitch Counts:** 23 wide x 86 high
**Approximate Finished Size:**
    14-count fabric:
    1⅝" wide x 6⅛" high

**Supplies**
- Zweigart® 14-Count Royal Blue Stitchband #7000-5
- Anchor® 6-Strand Embroidery Floss (1 skein each color)
- 1 spool Kreinik™ #4 Braid
- #24 Tapestry Needle
- Scissors

**Cross Stitch:** 2 strands
**Backstitch:** 1 strand
**Stitch Counts:** 93 wide x 79 high
**Approximate Finished Size:**
   14-count fabric: 6⅝" wide x 5⅝" high

**Supplies**
- Mouse Pad Kit
- Zweigart® 14-count
  Ice Blue Aida Fabric
- DMC® 6-Strand Embroidery Floss
  (1 skein each color)
- #24 Tapestry Needle

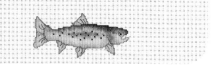

# I'd Rather Be Fishing Mouse Pad

### Design by Pam Kellogg

I'd rather be fishing. How many times have you heard an avid fisherman say that? A mouse pad with a fishing motif is an ideal gift for the fishermen on your gift list. If they can't be outdoors fishing, they can still enjoy their favorite hobby indoors, reminiscing about the big ones that got away!

As a companion to the mouse pad, stitch the design on a sweatshirt.

## DMC® 6-Strand Embroidery Floss

| | | | | | | |
|---|---|---|---|---|---|---|
| ■ | 310 | Black | 3 | 739 | Tan, ultra very light |
| 2 | 319 | Pistachio Green, very dark | ♡ | 760 | Salmon |
| m | 320 | Pistachio Green, medium | ★ | 761 | Salmon, light |
| ✎ | 367 | Pistachio Green, dark | ✕ | 890 | Pistachio Green, ultra dark |
| ♥ | 368 | Pistachio Green, light | ➔ | 3712 | Salmon, medium |
| ○ | 369 | Pistachio Green, very light | ↘ | 3713 | Salmon, very light |
| ✖ | 436 | Tan | ▼ | 3847 | Teal Green, dark |
| Z | 437 | Tan, light | ↻ | 3848 | Teal Green, medium |
| ♠ | 712 | Cream | ☆ | 3849 | Teal Green, light |
| ⌐ | 738 | Tan, very light | $ | 3865 | Winter White |

### General Instructions

When cross stitch is completed, follow manufacturer's instructions for mounting Aida fabric to mouse pad.

### Backstitch Instructions

Border: DMC 3712 Salmon, medium.
Grass: DMC 3849 Teal Green, light.
All other backstitch: DMC 310, Black

# Gifts for Friendship

## Anchor® 6-Strand Embroidery Floss

| | | |
|---|---|---|
| ✎ | 108 | Lavender, light |
| ♡ | 109 | Lavender, medium light |
| ✖ | 110 | Lavender, medium |
| 2 | 111 | Lavender, medium dark |
| ■ | 112 | Lavender, dark |
| // | 213 | Juniper, very light |
| ★ | 214 | Juniper, light |
| 3 | 215 | Juniper, medium light |
| ◖ | 216 | Juniper, medium |
| ∩ | 217 | Juniper, medium dark |
| ♥ | 218 | Juniper, dark |
| 4 | 302 | Citrus, medium light |
| ✖ | 303 | Citrus, medium |
| Z | 342 | Lilac, light |

## Backstitch Instructions

Violets and "T":
Anchor 112 Lavender, dark.
All other lettering:
Anchor 110 Lavender, medium.
Curlicues: Anchor 218
Juniper, dark.

## French Knot Instructions

• Lettering: Anchor 110
Lavender, medium.

# Friend Bookmark

## *Design by Pam Kellogg*

*Bookmarks are inexpensive gifts that can be personalized with a theme for the gift recipients. This lacy page-keeper features delicate violet blossoms surrounding a beautiful friendship verse. It's just perfect for that special friend.*

**Cross Stitch:** 2 strands
**Backstitch:** 1 strand
**French Knot:** 1 strand wrapped twice
**Stitch Counts:** 27 wide x 114 high
**Approximate Finished Size:**
    18-count: 1½" wide x 6¼" high

**Supplies**
● Crafter's Pride 18-Count White Lace-Trimmed
    Bookmark #40020W
● Anchor® 6-Strand Embroidery Floss
    (1 skein each color)
● #26 Tapestry Needle

**Cross Stitch:** 2 strands
**Backstitch:** 1 strand
**French Knot:** 2 strands wrapped twice
**Stitch Counts:** 91 wide x 67 high
**Approximate Finished Size:**
 28-count fabric stitched over two threads =
 14-count: 6½" wide x 4¾" high

**Supplies**
- Wichelt 28-Count Champagne Linen
  or 14-Count Aida
- DMC® 6-Strand Embroidery Floss
  (1 skein each color)
- Sudberry House #10161 Key Rack
- #24 Tapestry Needle

# Friendship Key Rack

### Design by Pam Kellogg

*The saying, "Friendship…doubles our joys and divides our sorrows" is so true. Double the joy in this decorative key rack by stitching two; give one to a friend and keep the second for yourself as a reminder of how important friendships are. In addition to being a gift that will be used and enjoyed for years, this piece will show how precious her friendship is to you.*

## General Instructions

This project was stitched over two threads on 28-count fabric in order for the design to fit within the key rack. If not using 28-count linen, a 14-count Aida would also fit in the key rack.

### DMC® 6-Strand Embroidery Floss

| | | | | | | | | |
|---|---|---|---|---|---|---|---|---|
| 3 | White | White | 4 | 798 | Delft Blue, dark | ¢ | 3078 | Golden Yellow, very light |
| ∩ | 434 | Brown, light | ⧋ | 799 | Delft Blue, medium | 2 | 3345 | Hunter Green, dark |
| ➜ | 435 | Brown, very light | ★ | 800 | Delft Blue, pale | ✖ | 3346 | Hunter Green |
| m | 436 | Tan | ♥ | 801 | Coffee Brown, dark | ♡ | 3347 | Yellow Green, medium |
| ✖ | 437 | Tan, light | $ | 809 | Delft Blue | ◢ | 3348 | Yellow Green, light |
| ♠ | 746 | Cream | ◖ | 895 | Hunter Green, very dark | ◨ | 3820 | Straw, dark |
| // | 772 | Yellow Green, very light | ☆ | 898 | Coffee Brown, very dark | ◜ | 3821 | Straw |
| ↘ | 796 | Royal Blue, dark | ■ | 938 | Coffee Brown, ultra dark | ✪ | 3822 | Straw, light |
| ◕ | 797 | Royal Blue | | | | | | |

### Backstitch Instructions

Blue flowers: DMC 796 Royal Blue, dark.
Leaves and stems: DMC 895 Hunter Green, very dark.
Centers of blue flowers: DMC 3820 Straw, dark.
All other backstitch: DMC 938 Coffee Brown, ultra dark.

### French Knot Instructions

• Verse: DMC 796 Royal Blue, dark.

**Cross Stitch:** 2 strands
**Backstitch:** 1 strand
**French Knot:** 2 strands wrapped once
**Stitch Counts:** 79 wide x 80 high
**Approximate Finished Size:**
   28-count fabric <u>stitched over two threads</u> =
   14-count: 5¾" wide x 5¾" high

**Supplies**
- DMC® 28-Count Antique White Evenweave
- DMC® 6-Strand Embroidery Floss
  (1 skein each color)
- Sudberry #99188 Square Oak Box
- #24 Tapestry Needle

# Friendship...
# a Gift From God

### Design by Roberta Madeleine

*This project is an inspiring and beautiful tribute to a wonderful friendship. Hearts represent that your friendship is from your heart. Florals represent the beauty of your friendship. The verse, "Friendship…a gift from God," says it all. Friends are truly a blessing from God to enjoy and treasure.*

## DMC® 6-Strand Embroidery Floss

| | | | | | | |
|---|---|---|---|---|---|---|
| □ | 225 | Shell Pink, ultra very light | ◥ | 987 | Forest Green, dark |
| ● | 304 | Christmas Red, medium | ╱ | 989 | Forest Green |
| L | 334 | Baby Blue, medium | 2 | 3348 | Yellow Green, light |
| ☆ | 445 | Lemon, light | ✖ | 3705 | Melon, dark |
| ▼ | 666 | Christmas Red, light | ♡ | 3708 | Melon, light |
| I | 725 | Topaz | ⊥ | 3840 | Lavender Blue, light |
| Z | 818 | Baby Pink | △ | 3852 | Straw, very dark |

### Backstitch Instructions
Hearts: DMC 956, Geranium.

### French Knot Instructions
• Placement noted on chart as those dots not within a square: DMC 956, Geranium.

# Gifts for
# Home Décor

# Wildflower Hand Towel Set

### Design by Laura Doyle

*You won't have to worry about these wildflowers wilting. Stitched on a crisp white lacy hand towel and washcloth, you can almost smell the flowers' fragrance. These colorful flowers will brighten up any bathroom. This duo would make a lovely gift set...if you can bear to give it away!*

**Cross Stitch:** 2 strands
**Stitch Counts:** 211 wide x 26 high (hand towel)
    122 wide x 26 high (washcloth)
**Approximate Finished Size:**
    14-count fabric: 15" wide x 1¾" high (hand towel)
    14-count fabric: 8⅝" wide x 1¾" high (washcloth)

**Supplies**
- Beautiful Accents™ 14-Count White Prefinished Lacy Hand Towel
- Beautiful Accents™ 14-Count White Aida Prefinished Lacy Washcloth
- Anchor® 6-Strand Embroidery Floss (1 skein each color)
- #24 Tapestry Needle

## Towel

Stitch complete motif centered on towel.

## Washcloth

Referring to the photograph as an additional guide, stitch motif from the start through the second sunflower centered on the washcloth.

### Anchor® 6-Strand Embroidery Floss

| | | | | | | | | | |
|---|---|---|---|---|---|---|---|---|---|
| · | 50 | China Rose, medium | ⬤ | 129 | Cobalt Blue | ❯ | 305 | Topaz, light |
| ♥ | 57 | Beauty Rose, medium | △ | 145 | Delft Blue, light | * | 307 | Topaz, medium |
| ⍦ | 62 | Magenta, medium | ✖ | 147 | Delft Blue, medium light | ● | 309 | Topaz, dark |
| — | 108 | Lavender, light | # | 243 | Grass Green, medium | ⚓ | 358 | Coffee |
| ⸳ | 110 | Lavender, medium | ◗ | 246 | Grass Green, very dark | ■ | 382 | Fudge, dark |
| ☐ | 128 | Cobalt Blue, light | ◌ | 293 | Jonquil, light | ◪ | 1044 | Grass Green, ultra dark |

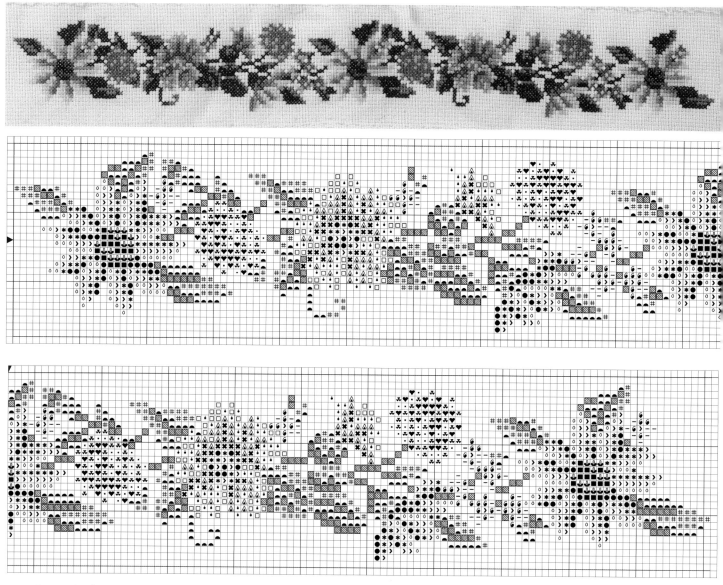

# Sports Afghan

### Designs by Mike Vickery

*Sports enthusiasts will feel like the most valuable player in your home with this winning afghan. Each square can also be stitched alone to be framed as a beautiful wall hanging for a den. Either way, this gift scores big points as a gift for that special man in your life.*

**Cross Stitch:** 2 strands
**Backstitch:** 1 strand

**Supplies**
- Zweigart® 14-Count Natural Hearthside Afghan with Hunter Green Stripes
- DMC® 6-Strand Embroidery Floss:
  - 1 skein each #310, #400, #402, #413, #414, #666, #720, #783, and #3823
  - 2 skeins each #301, #319, #367, #368, #644, #721, #722, #725, #727, #3078, #3776, #3799, and #3825
  - 3 skeins #822
  - 6 skeins white
- #24 Tapestry Needle

# Afghan Layout

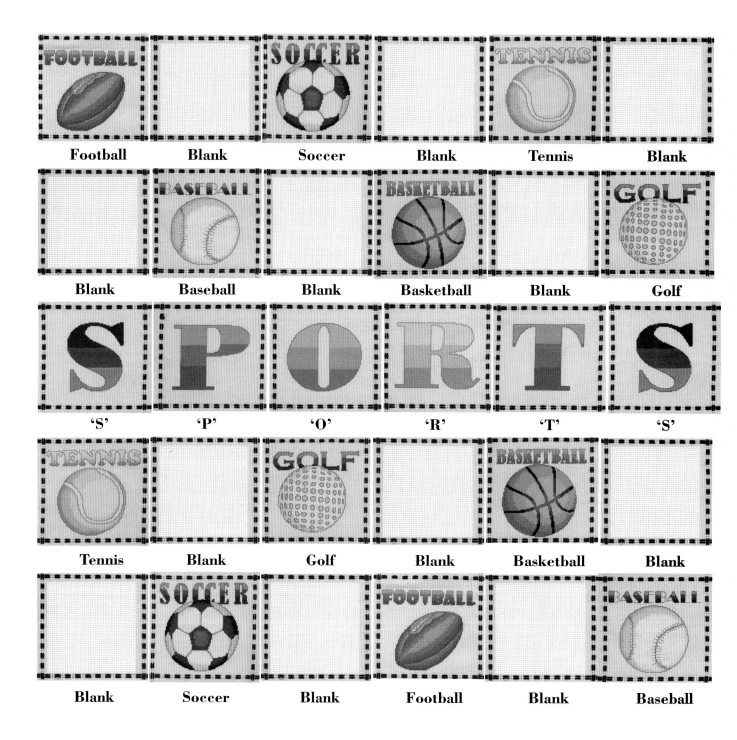

| | | | | | |
|---|---|---|---|---|---|
| Football | Blank | Soccer | Blank | Tennis | Blank |
| Blank | Baseball | Blank | Basketball | Blank | Golf |
| 'S' | 'P' | 'O' | 'R' | 'T' | 'S' |
| Tennis | Blank | Golf | Blank | Basketball | Blank |
| Blank | Soccer | Blank | Football | Blank | Baseball |

# Football Panel

**Stitch Count:** 91 wide x 80 high
**Approximate Finished Size:** 14-count fabric: 6⅝" wide x 5¾" high

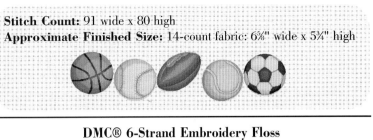

## DMC® 6-Strand Embroidery Floss

| | | | | | | |
|---|---|---|---|---|---|---|
| · | White | White | < | 402 | Mahogany, very light |
| ◔ | 301 | Mahogany, medium | + | 822 | Beige Gray, light |
| ✗ | 400 | Mahogany, dark | # | 3776 | Mahogany, light |

## Backstitch Instructions

All backstitch: DMC 3799 Pewter Gray, very dark.

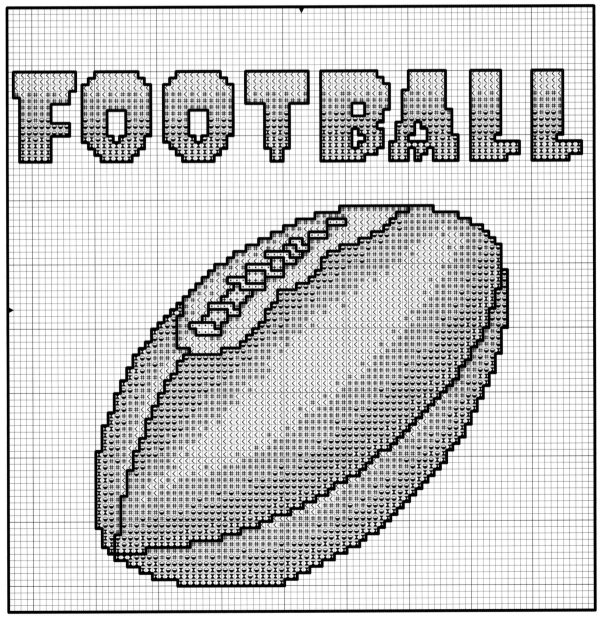

©2002 Zweigart®

# Soccer Panel

**Stitch Count:** 86 wide x 89 high
**Approximate Finished Size:** 14-count fabric: 6⅜" wide x 6⅜" high

### DMC® 6-Strand Embroidery Floss

| | | | | | |
|---|---|---|---|---|---|
| · | White | White | ✳ | 413 | Pewter Gray, dark |
| ↑ | 310 | Black | c | 414 | Steel Gray, dark |
| ✖ | 319 | Pistachio Green, very dark | ▾ | 644 | Beige Gray, medium |
| 8 | 367 | Pistachio Green, dark | + | 822 | Beige Gray, light |
| □ | 368 | Pistachio Green, light | | | |

### Backstitch Instructions
All backstitch: DMC 3799
Pewter Gray, very dark.

©2002 Zweigart®

◆ ◢ ◗ ♥ ✖ ★ *Gifts to Cross Stitch*

# Tennis Panel

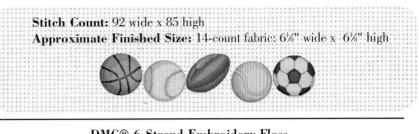

**Stitch Count:** 92 wide x 85 high
**Approximate Finished Size:** 14-count fabric: 6⅝" wide x 6⅛" high

### DMC® 6-Strand Embroidery Floss

| | | | | | |
|---|---|---|---|---|---|
| Y | 725 | Topaz | ( | 3078 | Golden Yellow, very light |
| S | 727 | Topaz, very light | ‡ | 3823 | Yellow, ultra pale |
| ◆ | 783 | Topaz, medium | | | |

## Backstitch Instructions

All backstitch: DMC 3799 Pewter Gray, very dark.

# Baseball Panel

**Stitch Count:** 91 wide x 81 high
**Approximate Finished Size:** 14-count fabric: 6½" wide x 5¾" high

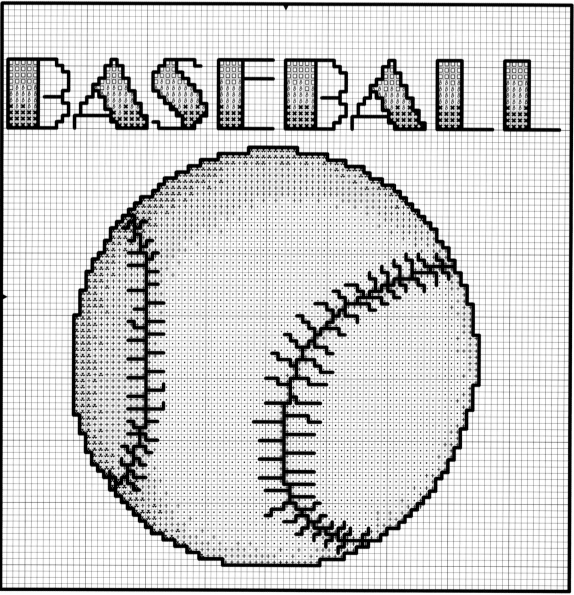

## DMC® 6-Strand Embroidery Floss

| | | | | | | |
|---|---|---|---|---|---|---|
| · | White | White | □ | 368 | Pistachio Green, light |
| ✗ | 319 | Pistachio Green, very dark | ♣ | 644 | Beige Gray, medium |
| | | | + | 822 | Beige Gray, light |
| 8 | 367 | Pistachio Green, dark | | | |

### Backstitch Instructions

"Stitched" lines within baseball: DMC 666 Christmas Red, bright.

All other backstitch: DMC 3799 Pewter Gray, very dark.

©2002 Zweigart®

# Basketball Panel

**Stitch Count:** 88 wide x 87 high
**Approximate Finished Size:** 14-count fabric: 6⅓" wide x 6¼" high

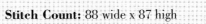

## DMC® 6-Strand Embroidery Floss

| | | | | | | |
|---|---|---|---|---|---|---|
| ↑ | 310 | Black | | ⊕ | 721 | Orange Spice, medium |
| ✳ | 413 | Pewter Gray, dark | | 3 | 722 | Orange Spice, light |
| C | 414 | Steel Gray, dark | | / | 3825 | Pumpkin, pale |
| ▲ | 720 | Orange Spice, dark | | | | |

## Backstitch Instructions

All backstitch: DMC 3799 Pewter Gray, very dark

©2002 Zweigart®

# Golf Panel

**Stitch Count:** 85 wide x 81 high
**Approximate Finished Size:** 14-count fabric: 6⅛" wide x 5¾" high

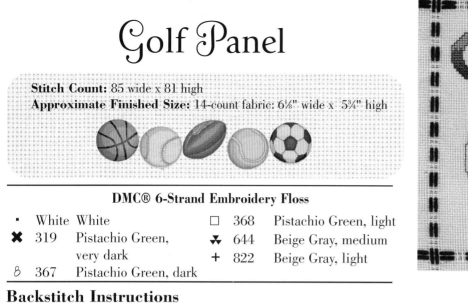

### DMC® 6-Strand Embroidery Floss

| | | | | | | |
|---|---|---|---|---|---|---|
| · | White | White | □ | 368 | Pistachio Green, light |
| ✖ | 319 | Pistachio Green, very dark | ▼ | 644 | Beige Gray, medium |
| 8 | 367 | Pistachio Green, dark | + | 822 | Beige Gray, light |

## Backstitch Instructions

All backstitch: DMC 3799 Pewter Gray, very dark.

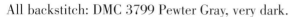

# "S" Panel

**Stitch Count:** 55 wide x 69 high
**Approximate Finished Size:**
14-count fabric: 4" wide x 5" high

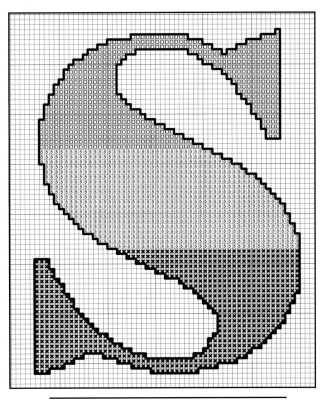

## DMC® 6-Strand Embroidery Floss

| | | |
|---|---|---|
| ✖ | 319 | Pistachio Green, very dark |
| 8 | 367 | Pistachio Green, dark |
| □ | 368 | Pistachio Green, light |

## Backstitch Instructions

All backstitch: DMC 3799 Pewter Gray, very dark.

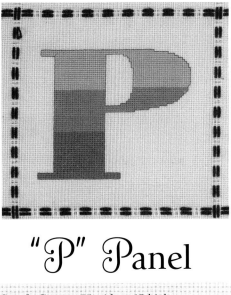

# "P" Panel

**Stitch Count:** 75 wide x 65 high
**Approximate Finished Size:**
14-count fabric: 5⅜" wide x 4⅝" high

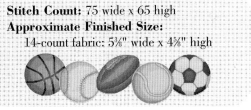

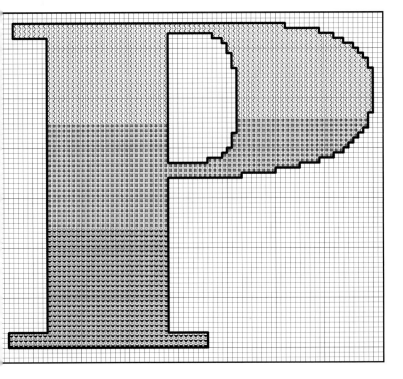

## DMC® 6-Strand Embroidery Floss

| | | |
|---|---|---|
| ● | 301 | Mahogany, medium |
| < | 402 | Mahogany, very light |
| # | 3776 | Mahogany, light |

## Backstitch Instructions

All backstitch: DMC 3799 Pewter Gray, very dark.

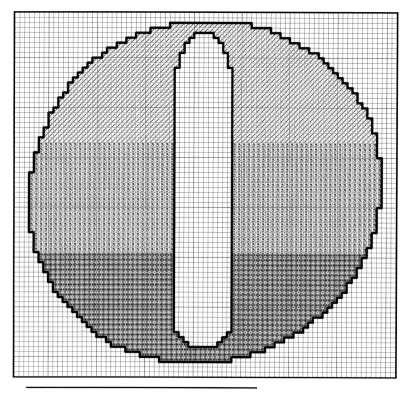

## DMC® 6-Strand Embroidery Floss

⊕　721　Orange Spice, medium

З　722　Orange Spice, light

╱　3825　Pumpkin, pale

## Backstitch Instructions

All backstitch: DMC 3799 Pewter Gray, very dark.

## "R" Panel

**Stitch Count:** 84 wide x 65 high

**Approximate Finished Size:**
14-count fabric: 6" wide x 4⅝" high

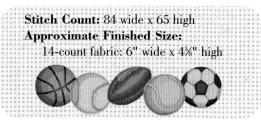

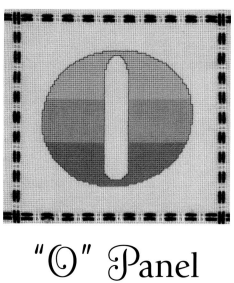

## "O" Panel

**Stitch Count:** 73 wide x 67 high

**Approximate Finished Size:**
14-count fabric: 5¼" wide x 4¾" high

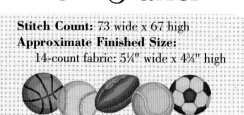

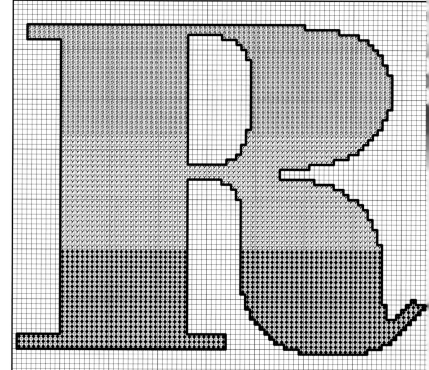

## DMC® 6-Strand Embroidery Floss

Y　725　Topaz

S　727　Topaz, very light

◆　783　Topaz, medium

## Backstitch Instructions

All backstitch: DMC 3799 Pewter Gray, very dark.

# "T" Panel

**Stitch Count:** 69 wide x 66 high
**Approximate Finished Size:**
14-count fabric: 5" wide x 4¾" high

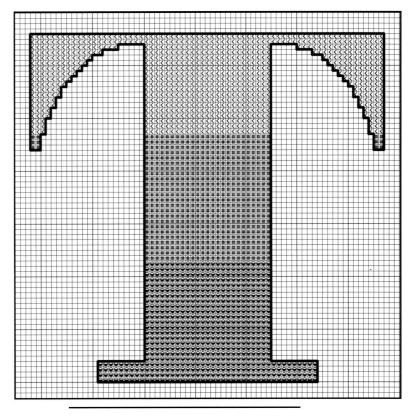

**DMC® 6-Strand Embroidery Floss**

◓   301     Mahogany, medium
<   402     Mahogany, very light
\#   3776   Mahogany, light

## Backstitch Instructions

All backstitch: DMC 3799 Pewter Gray, very dark.

# Cheese and Grapes Kitchen Set

### Designs by Pam Kellogg

*The cheese and grapes combination adds just a hint of old-world charm to this coordinating kitchen set. The motif adorns a cheese board with coordinating potholder and towel—three lovely gifts that will be appreciated and used for years.*

**Stitch Counts:** 74 wide x 76 high (cheese board)
  63 wide x 44 high (potholder)
  57 wide x 67 high (towel)
**Approximate Finished Size:**
  14-count fabric: 4" wide x 4⅛" high (cheese board)
  14-count fabric: 4½" wide x 3⅛" high (potholder)
  14-count fabric: 4" wide x 4¾" high (towel)

**Supplies**
- Sudberry House Cheese Board #95290
- Charles Craft Showcase Potholder with White 14-Count Aida Insert
- Charles Craft Showcase Huck Towel with White 14-Count Aida Insert
- Anchor® 6-Strand Embroidery Floss (2 skeins each color)
- Charles Craft White 14-Count Aida
- #24 Tapestry Needle

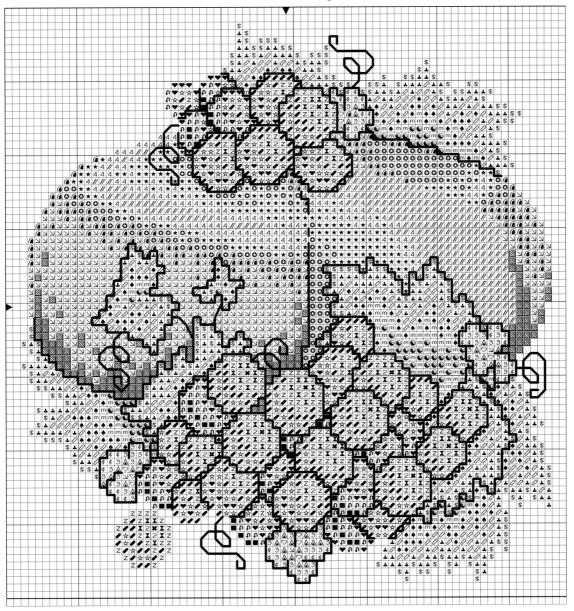

©2002 Charles Craft Inc.

## General Instructions

The keycode is for all three designs. Be aware that some symbols will not be in all three designs.

## Backstitch Instructions

Grapes: Anchor 150 Delft Blue, dark.

Leaves and curlicues: Anchor 218 Juniper, dark.

Right side of cheese on towel design: Anchor 307 Topaz, medium.

Rest of cheese: Anchor 308 Topaz, medium dark.

Flowers: Anchor 333 Blaze, medium light.

*(Keycode on next page.)*

## Anchor® 6-Strand Embroidery Floss

| | | | | | | | | | |
|---|---|---|---|---|---|---|---|---|---|
| ✖ | White | White | ↘ | 214 | Juniper, light | ↘ | 307 | Topaz, medium |
| ✗ | 128 | Cobalt Blue, light | ∅ | 215 | Juniper, medium light | ▨ | 308 | Topaz, medium dark |
| ✎ | 130 | Cobalt Blue, medium light | ♠ | 216 | Juniper, medium | ¢ | 328 | Melon, light |
| ✿ | 145 | Delft Blue, light | m | 217 | Juniper, medium dark | 3 | 329 | Melon |
| ☆ | 146 | Delft Blue | ☢ | 218 | Juniper, dark | ⚠ | 330 | Melon, dark |
| ♥ | 147 | Delft Blue, medium light | ★ | 293 | Jonquil, light | ♡ | 332 | Blaze, light |
| ♫ | 149 | Delft Blue, medium dark | 4 | 300 | Citrus, light | // | 386 | Citrus, very light |
| ■ | 150 | Delft Blue, dark | ✪ | 305 | Topaz, light | 2 | 1037 | Sea Blue, very light |
| $ | 213 | Juniper, very light | ◖ | 306 | Topaz, medium light | | | |

### Potholder Design

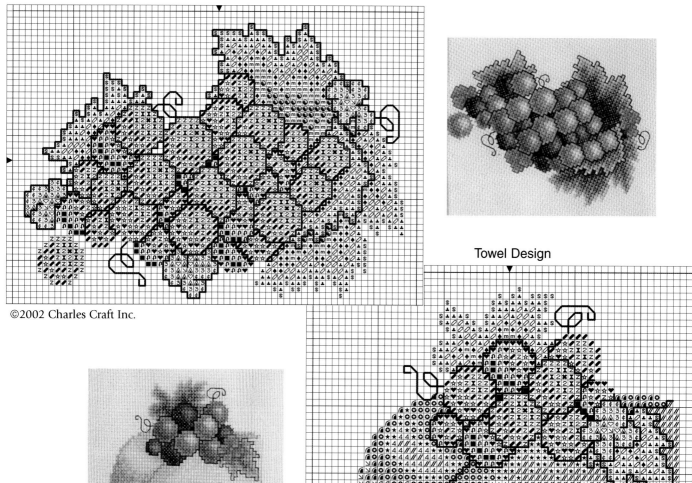

©2002 Charles Craft Inc.

### Towel Design

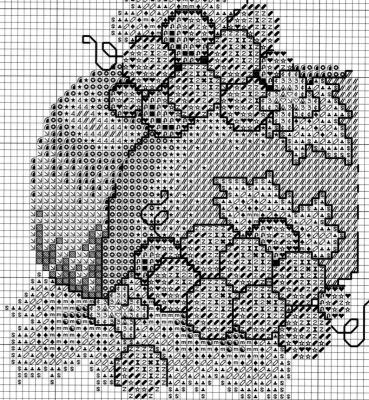

# Blue Roses Bedroom Set

### Design by Pam Kellogg

*Blue roses provide elegance and splendor for making a spectacular bedroom. Start with a bedside table topper trimmed in cluny lace and adorned with blue roses. Add custom prefinished pillowcases with the same blue rose theme. Throw in a coordinating personalized pillow sham also trimmed in cluny lace. And for the finishing touch, add a Battenburg laced doily with blue roses to place on a serving tray or nearby dresser.*

**Cross Stitch:** 3 strands
**Backstitch:** 1 strand
**Stitch Counts:** 102 wide x 97 high
  (table topper)
**Approximate Finished Size:**
  10-count fabric: 10⅛" wide x 9⅝" high

**Supplies**
- Beautiful Accents™ 10-Count White Prefinished Tula® Table Topper
- DMC® 6-Strand Embroidery Floss (2 skeins each color)
- #22 Tapestry Needle

# Blue Roses Table Topper

*Design by Pam Kellogg*

## DMC® 6-Strand Embroidery Floss

| | | | | | |
|---|---|---|---|---|---|
| O | White | White | ♡ | 827 | Blue, very light |
| ✎ | 162 | Blue, very light | 2 | 828 | Blue, ultra very light |
| m | 772 | Yellow Green, very light | ♥ | 895 | Hunter Green, very dark |
| ✗ | 813 | Blue, light | ⊘ | 3345 | Hunter Green, dark |
| ■ | 824 | Blue, very dark | ➜ | 3346 | Hunter Green |
| 4 | 825 | Blue, dark | $ | 3347 | Yellow Green, medium |
| ☆ | 826 | Blue, medium | ✖ | 3348 | Yellow Green, light |

### Backstitch Instructions

Roses: DMC 824 Blue, very dark.
Leaves: DMC 895 Hunter Green, very dark.

# Blue Roses Alphabet

### Design by Pam Kellogg

**DMC® 6-Strand Embroidery Floss**

| | | |
|---|---|---|
| ✘ | 813 | Blue, light |
| ■ | 824 | Blue, very dark |
| 4 | 825 | Blue, dark |
| ☆ | 826 | Blue, medium |
| ♡ | 827 | Blue, very light |

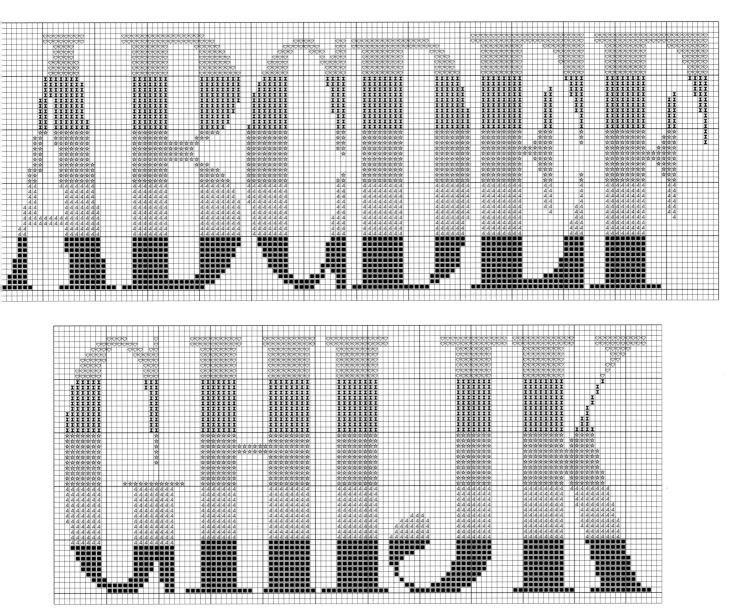

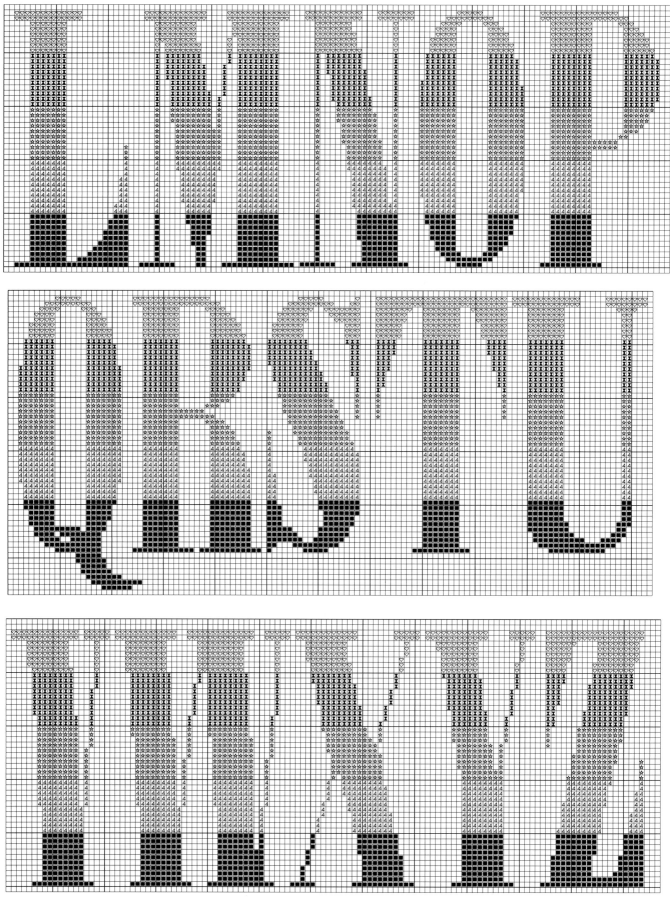

# Blue Roses Pillow Sham

### Design by Pam Kellogg

*(Instructions and keycode on next page.)*

**Cross Stitch:** 2 strands
**Backstitch:** 1 strand
**Stitch Counts:** 147 wide x 110 high
**Approximate Finished Size:**
    14-count fabric: 10½" wide x 7¾" high

**Supplies**
- Beautiful Accents™ 14-Count White Aida Prefinished Pillow Sham
- DMC® 6-Strand Embroidery Floss (1 skein each color)
- #24 Tapestry Needle

## General Instructions

Refer to Blue Roses Alphabet, page 73, and choose three initials to go on the sham with the design. Center the design and initials on sham.

## Backstitch Instructions

Roses: DMC 824 Blue, very dark.
Leaves: DMC 895 Hunter Green, very dark.

### DMC® 6-Strand Embroidery Floss

| | | | | | | | | |
|---|---|---|---|---|---|---|---|---|
| O | White | White | 4 | 825 | Blue, dark | ⊘ | 3345 | Hunter Green, dark |
| ◢ | 162 | Blue, very light | ☆ | 826 | Blue, medium | ➜ | 3346 | Hunter Green |
| m | 772 | Yellow Green, very light | ♡ | 827 | Blue, very light | $ | 3347 | Yellow Green, medium |
| ✕ | 813 | Blue, light | 2 | 828 | Blue, ultra very light | ✖ | 3348 | Yellow Green, light |
| ■ | 824 | Blue, very dark | ♥ | 895 | Hunter Green, very dark | | | |

©2002 X-Stitch Enterprises

# Blue Roses Pillowcase and Doily

### *Design by Pam Kellogg*

## General Instructions

The same design fits on the prefinished pillowcase and doily.

## Backstitch Instructions

Roses: DMC 824 Blue, very dark.
Leaves: DMC 895 Hunter Green, very dark.

**Cross Stitch:** 2 strands
**Backstitch:** 1 strand
**Stitch Counts:** 135 wide x 38 high
**Approximate Finished Size:**
14-count fabric: 9⅝" wide x 2⅝" high

**Supplies**
- Beautiful Accents™ 14-Count White Aida Prefinished Pillowcase
- Beautiful Accents™ 14-Count White Battenburg Doily
- DMC® 6-Strand Embroidery Floss (2 skeins each color per pillowcase and doily set)
- #24 Tapestry Needle

### DMC® 6-Strand Embroidery Floss

| | | | | | | |
|---|---|---|---|---|---|---|
| O | White | White | ♡ | 827 | Blue, very light |
| ◢ | 162 | Blue, very light | 2 | 828 | Blue, ultra very light |
| m | 772 | Yellow Green, very light | ♥ | 895 | Hunter Green, very dark |
| X | 813 | Blue, light | ∅ | 3345 | Hunter Green, dark |
| ■ | 824 | Blue, very dark | ➡ | 3346 | Hunter Green |
| 4 | 825 | Blue, dark | $ | 3347 | Yellow Green, medium |
| ☆ | 826 | Blue, medium | ✖ | 3348 | Yellow Green, light |

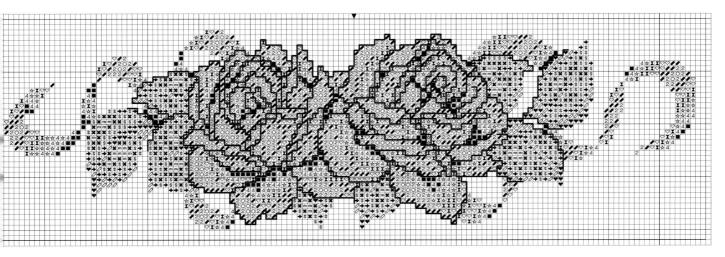

# Four Seasons Towels

### Designs by Pam Kellogg

*Celebrate the beauty of nature's four seasons! These towels, with colorful checkered borders and easy-to-stitch 8-count Aida inserts, are the ideal way to showcase fruit, no matter what time of year they are harvested.*

**Cross Stitch:** 4 strands
**Backstitch:** 1 strand
**Stitch Counts:** 85 wide x 22 high (all designs)
**Approximate Finished Size:**
   8-count fabric: 10⅝" wide x 2¾" high

**Supplies**
- 4 Zweigart® 8-Count White Cottage Huck Towels
- DMC® 6-Strand Embroidery Floss
  (2 skeins each color per towel design)
- #20 Tapestry Needle

©2002 Zweigart®

# Spring Towel

## DMC® 6-Strand Embroidery Floss

| | | | | | | |
|---|---|---|---|---|---|---|
| ♡ | 309 | Rose, dark | | • | 818 | Baby Pink |
| ◧ | 326 | Rose, very dark | | ✕ | 895 | Hunter Green, very dark |
| ➜ | 335 | Rose | | ✚ | 898 | Coffee Brown, very dark |
| ▼ | 433 | Brown, medium | | 3 | 899 | Rose, medium |
| ¢ | 434 | Brown, light | | ? | 936 | Avocado Green, very dark |
| // | 469 | Avocado Green | | ◖ | 937 | Avocado Green, medium |
| ★ | 470 | Avocado Green, light | | ▣ | 3326 | Rose, light |
| 4 | 471 | Avocado Green, very light | | m | 3345 | Hunter Green, dark |
| ▼ | 472 | Avocado Green, ultra light | | ◕ | 3346 | Hunter Green |
| ↘ | 772 | Yellow Green, very light | | 2 | 3347 | Yellow Green, medium |
| ⌗ | 776 | Pink, medium | | ♥ | 3348 | Yellow Green, light |
| ☆ | 801 | Coffee Brown, dark | | | | |

## Backstitch Instructions

Strawberries: DMC 326 Rose, very dark.
Watermelon: DMC 895 Hunter Green, very dark.

Strawberry tops and leaves: DMC 935 Avocado Green, dark.
Stems, verse, and curlicues: DMC 938 Coffee Brown, ultra dark.

©2002 Zweigart®

# Summer Towel

## DMC® 6-Strand Embroidery Floss

| | | | | | | |
|---|---|---|---|---|---|---|
| ⌀ | 304 | Christmas Red, medium | | ⊥ | 801 | Coffee Brown, dark |
| 2 | 319 | Pistachio Green, very dark | | ■ | 890 | Pistachio Green, ultra dark |
| ⌂ | 320 | Pistachio Green, medium | | ◩ | 900 | Burnt Orange, dark |
| ◖ | 321 | Christmas Red | | ☋ | 3340 | Apricot, medium |
| ♥ | 367 | Pistachio Green, dark | | ✖ | 3341 | Apricot |
| ◣ | 368 | Pistachio Green, light | | ☆ | 3705 | Melon, dark |
| m | 369 | Pistachio Green, very light | | ⬭ | 3706 | Melon, medium |
| = | 433 | Brown, medium | | ➜ | 3801 | Christmas Red, light |
| ✗ | 498 | Christmas Red, very dark | | // | 3823 | Yellow, very pale |
| 3 | 666 | Christmas Red, bright | | ⬎ | 3825 | Orange Spice, very light |
| · | 746 | Off White | | ★ | 3855 | Autumn Gold, light |

## Backstitch Instructions

Cherries: DMC 816 Garnet.

Leaves: DMC 890 Pistachio Green, ultra dark.

Stems, verse, and curlicues: DMC 938 Coffee Brown, ultra dark.

Peach: DMC 3340 Apricot, medium.

©2002 Zweigart®

# Autumn Towel

## DMC® 6-Strand Embroidery Floss

| | | | | | |
|---|---|---|---|---|---|
| ♡ | 209 | Lavender, dark | 3 | 552 | Violet, medium |
| ★ | 210 | Lavender, medium | ✗ | 553 | Violet |
| // | 211 | Lavender, light | 2 | 745 | Yellow, light pale |
| ⋒ | 301 | Mahogany, medium | • | 746 | Off White |
| ■ | 400 | Mahogany, dark | ➜ | 801 | Coffee Brown, dark |
| ? | 433 | Brown, medium | $ | 898 | Coffee Brown, very dark |
| ✚ | 434 | Brown, light | ✖ | 935 | Avocado Green, dark |
| ◇◇ | 435 | Brown, very light | ⅄ | 936 | Avocado Green, very dark |
| 4 | 469 | Avocado Green | ⋀ | 937 | Avocado Green, medium |
| ♠ | 470 | Avocado Green, light | ♥ | 3853 | Autumn Gold, dark |
| ⊙ | 471 | Avocado Green, very light | m | 3854 | Autumn Gold, medium |
| ☆ | 472 | Avocado Green, ultra light | ✐ | 3855 | Autumn Gold, light |
| ▧ | 550 | Violet, very dark | | | |

## Backstitch Instructions

Pumpkin: DMC 400 Mahogany, dark.
Grapes: DMC 550 Violet, very dark.

Leaves and stems: DMC 935 Avocado Green, dark.
Curlicues and verse: DMC 938 Coffee Brown, ultra dark.

© 2002 Zweigart®

# Winter Towel

## DMC® 6-Strand Embroidery Floss

| | | | | | |
|---|---|---|---|---|---|
| 3 | 321 | Christmas Red | ◪ | 895 | Hunter Green, very dark |
| ⊘ | 433 | Brown, medium | m | 898 | Coffee Brown, very dark |
| ■ | 608 | Bright Orange | 2 | 3345 | Hunter Green, dark |
| ◢ | 666 | Christmas Red, light | ✖ | 3346 | Hunter Green |
| ↘ | 740 | Tangerine | ☆ | 3347 | Yellow Green, medium |
| ◖ | 741 | Tangerine, medium | ♥ | 3348 | Yellow Green, light |
| ? | 742 | Tangerine, light | ✘ | 3705 | Melon, dark |
| ⊥ | 743 | Yellow, medium | // | 3706 | Melon, medium |
| $ | 744 | Yellow, pale | ✪ | 3708 | Melon, light |
| ★ | 745 | Yellow, light pale | ♡ | 3801 | Rose |
| ∩ | 772 | Yellow Green, very light | 4 | 3823 | Yellow, very |
| ⟁ | 801 | Coffee Brown, dark | | | |

## Backstitch Instructions

Berries: DMC 498 Christmas Red, very dark.
Orange: DMC 740 Tangerine.

Leaves: DMC 895 Hunter Green, very dark.
Verse, stems, and curlicues: DMC 938 Coffee Brown, ultra dark.

# Flower-of-the-Month Afghan

### Designs by Pam Kellogg

*Celebrate each month by stitching a different flower. When you're finished, you'll have an afghan representing the flowers of each month. Or, stitch an individual flower for a birthday gift. Finish it as a framed picture or pillow—or mount in a serving tray. With 12 different flower designs shown here, the possibilities are many!*

**Cross Stitch:** 2 strands
**Backstitch:** 1 strand
**French Knot:** 1 strand wrapped twice
**Stitch Counts:** 84 wide x 84 high
        (each flower motif)
**Approximate Finished Size:**
   18-count fabric stitched over one thread:
   4⅝" wide x 4⅝" high (each flower motif)

**Supplies**
- Zweigart® 18-Count Natural Anne Cloth Afghan
- DMC® 6-Strand Embroidery Floss (2 skeins each color per flower)
- Kreinik™ #4 Braid
- #26 Tapestry Needle

# Afghan Layout

Seven rows blank at top.

Blank  January  Blank  February  Blank  March  Blank

Seven rows blank across.

Blank  April  Blank  May  Blank  June  Blank

Seven rows blank across.

Blank  July  Blank  August  Blank  September  Blank

Seven rows blank across.

Blank  October  Blank  November  Blank  December  Blank

Seven rows blank at bottom.

## General Instructions

This afghan is stitched over one thread, not two, in order to fit within the space of each square.

The afghan contains seven rows across and nine rows down. Leave the top and bottom horizontal rows blank. Leave the left and right vertical rows blank. Begin stitching on the second row in the second square with the flower for January. Skip the next square. Stitch the flower for February in the fourth square. Skip the next square. Stitch the flower for March in the sixth square. Leave the next row blank. Begin in the fourth row, second square and stitch the flower for April. Skip the next square. Stitch the flower for May in the next square. Skip the following square. Stitch the flower for June in the next square. Leave the next row blank. Repeat procedure for stitching remaining flowers going in the order of the months.

When cross stitch is completed, fringe as desired.

# January Carnation

| DMC® 6-Strand Embroidery Floss | | | | | |
|---|---|---|---|---|---|
| · | White | White | Z | 369 | Pistachio Green, very light |
| ☆ | 309 | Rose, Deep | ∩ | 776 | Pink, medium |
| 3 | 319 | Pistachio Green, very dark | ♥ | 818 | Baby Pink |
| ♡ | 320 | Pistachio Green, medium | 2 | 819 | Baby Pink, light |
| ✕ | 326 | Rose, very dark | ◖ | 890 | Pistachio Green, ultra dark |
| ✦ | 335 | Rose | :: | 899 | Rose, medium |
| ✪ | 367 | Pistachio Green, dark | ✖ | 3326 | Rose, light |
| ★ | 368 | Pistachio Green, light | **Kreinik™ #4 Braid** | | |
| | | | ■ | 210 | Gold Dust |

## Backstitch Instructions

Flowers and lettering: DMC 326 Rose, very dark.

Greenery: DMC 890 Pistachio Green, ultra dark.

Flower centers: DMC 3822 Straw, light.

Border: Kreinik #4 Braid 210 Gold Dust.

## French Knot Instructions

• Lettering: DMC 326 Rose, very dark.

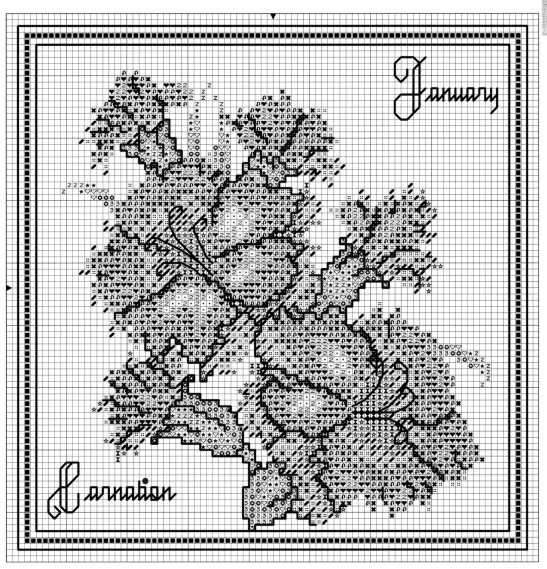

# February Violet

| DMC® 6-strand Embroidery Floss | | | | | |
|---|---|---|---|---|---|
| ★ | 164 | Green | ♡ | 987 | Forest Green, dark |
| ∩ | 209 | Lavender, dark | ✖ | 988 | Forest Green, medium |
| ✖ | 210 | Lavender, medium | Z | 989 | Forest Green |
| 2 | 211 | Lavender, light | ✪ | 3820 | Straw, dark |
| ⊘ | 552 | Violet, medium | m | 3821 | Straw |
| ♥ | 553 | Violet | ◢ | 3822 | Straw, light |
| ◖ | 986 | Forest Green, very dark | **Kreinik™ #4 Braid** | | |
| | | | ▧ | 210 | Gold Dust |

## Backstitch Instructions

Violets and lettering:
DMC 550 Violet, very dark.
Stems: DMC 986 Forest Green, very dark.

Border: Kreinik #4 Braid 210 Gold Dust.

## French Knot Instructions

• Lettering: DMC 550 Violet, very dark.

©2002 Zweigart®

# March Daffodil

**DMC® 6-Strand Embroidery Floss**

| | | |
|---|---|---|
| ■ | 740 | Tangerine |
| // | 741 | Tangerine, medium |
| ♥ | 742 | Tangerine, light |
| 3 | 743 | Yellow, medium |
| ➔ | 744 | Yellow, pale |
| m | 745 | Yellow, light pale |
| 2 | 746 | Off White |
| ♡ | 772 | Yellow Green, very light |
| ✖ | 895 | Hunter Green, very dark |
| ☆ | 3345 | Hunter Green, dark |
| ◢ | 3346 | Hunter Green |
| 4 | 3347 | Yellow Green, medium |
| ◖ | 3348 | Yellow Green, light |
| ✪ | 3823 | Yellow, very pale |

**Kreinik™ #4 Braid**

| | | |
|---|---|---|
| ▨ | 210 | Gold Dust |

## Backstitch Instructions

Daffodil petals: DMC 742 Tangerine, light.

Daffodil centers: DMC 745 Yellow, light pale.

Greenery: DMC 895 Hunter Green, very dark.

Border: Kreinik #4 Braid 210 Gold Dust.

All other backstitch: DMC 740 Tangerine.

## French Knot Instructions

• Lettering: DMC 740 Tangerine.
• Daffodil centers: Two strands wrapped twice, DMC 745 Yellow, light pale.

# April Sweet Pea

**DMC® 6-Strand Embroidery Floss**

| | | |
|---|---|---|
| o | White | White |
| m | 319 | Pistachio Green, very dark |
| 2 | 320 | Pistachio Green, medium |
| ♥ | 367 | Pistachio Green, dark |
| ✗ | 368 | Pistachio Green, light |
| ∅ | 369 | Pistachio Green, very light |
| ✖ | 718 | Plum |
| ■ | 890 | Pistachio Green, ultra dark |
| z | 917 | Plum, medium |
| ♡ | 3607 | Plum, light |
| ◢ | 3608 | Plum, very light |
| 3 | 3609 | Plum, ultra light |
| ★ | 3689 | Mauve, light |

**Kreinik™ #4 Braid**

| | | |
|---|---|---|
| ◨ | 210 | Gold Dust |

## Backstitch Instructions
Greenery: DMC 890
Pistachio Green, ultra dark.
Flowers and lettering: DMC 915
Plum, dark.

Border: Kreinik #4 Braid 210
Gold Dust.

## French Knot Instructions
• Lettering: DMC 915 Plum, dark.

©2002 ZWEIGART®

◆ ◢ ∅ ♥ ✗ ★  *Gifts to Cross Stitch*

# May Lily of the Valley

| **DMC® 6-Strand Embroidery Floss** | | |
|---|---|---|
| ♡ | White | White |
| // | 318 | Steel Gray, light |
| ★ | 415 | Pearl Gray |
| ⬮ | 469 | Avocado Green |
| ก | 470 | Avocado Green, light |
| ♥ | 471 | Avocado Green, very light |
| 2 | 472 | Avocado Green, ultra light |
| 3 | 676 | Old Gold, light |
| ✖ | 729 | Old Gold, medium |
| z | 762 | Pearl Gray, very light |
| ■ | 934 | Black Avocado Green |
| 4 | 935 | Avocado Green, dark |
| ⧗ | 936 | Avocado Green, very dark |
| m | 937 | Avocado Green, medium |
| **Kreinik™ #4 Braid** | | |
| ▧ | 210 | Gold Dust |

**Backstitch Instructions**

Flowers: DMC 414 Steel Gray, dark.

Lettering: DMC 729 Old Gold, medium.

Greenery: DMC 934 Black Avocado Green.

Border: Kreinik #4 Braid 210 Gold Dust.

## French Knot Instructions

• Lettering: DMC 729 Old Gold, medium.

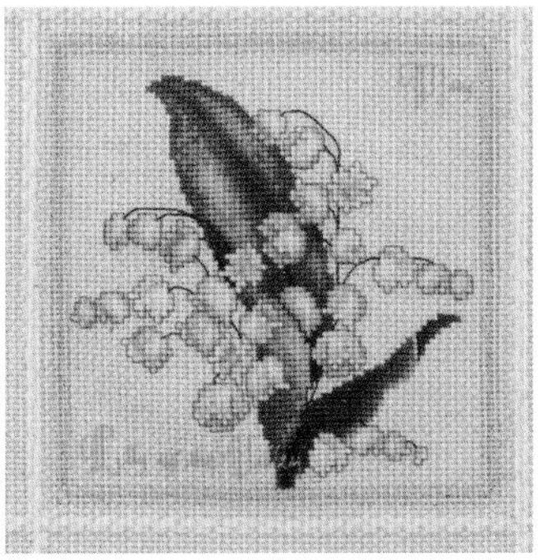

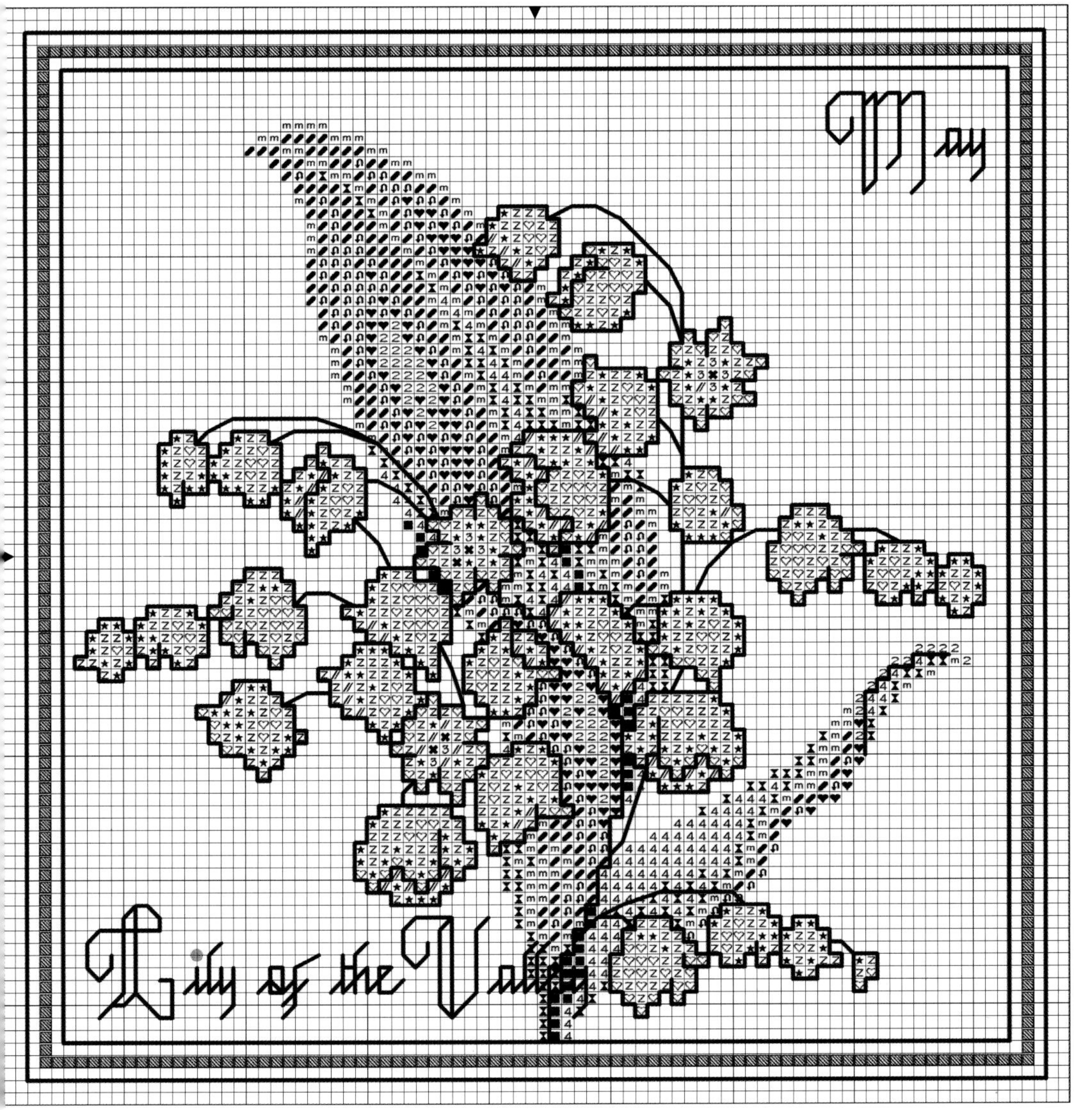

# June Rose

## DMC® 6-Strand Embroidery Floss

| | | | | | | |
|---|---|---|---|---|---|---|
| ⌐ | 304 | Christmas Red, medium | ★ | 666 | Christmas Red, bright |
| 3 | 319 | Pistachio Green, very dark | m | 815 | Garnet, medium |
| ⌐ | 320 | Pistachio Green, medium | ◣ | 816 | Garnet |
| ⌐ | 321 | Christmas Red | + | 890 | Pistachio Green, ultra dark |
| → | 367 | Pistachio Green, dark | ■ | 936 | Avocado Green, very dark |
| ✪ | 368 | Pistachio Green, light | ⊾ | 937 | Avocado Green, medium |
| // | 369 | Pistachio Green, very light | ✖ | 3705 | Melon, dark |
| ↑ | 469 | Avocado Green | $ | 3706 | Melon, medium |
| ☆ | 470 | Avocado Green, light | ♥ | 3708 | Melon, light |
| ☯ | 471 | Avocado Green, very light | ¢ | 3801 | Christmas Red, light |
| 4 | 472 | Avocado Green, ultra light | **Kreinik™ #4 Braid** | | |
| 2 | 498 | Christmas Red, dark | ▨ | 210 | Gold Dust |

## Backstitch Instructions

Rose: DMC 814 Garnet, dark.
Border: Kreinik #4 Braid 210 Gold Dust.

# July Larkspur

**DMC® 6-Strand Embroidery Floss**

| | | |
|---|---|---|
| ✪ | 676 | Old Gold, light |
| 4 | 677 | Old Gold, very light |
| ♡ | 772 | Yellow Green, very light |
| z | 775 | Baby Blue, very light |
| ◖ | 797 | Royal Blue |
| ∩ | 798 | Delft Blue, dark |
| ♥ | 799 | Delft Blue, medium |
| ✖ | 800 | Delft Blue, pale |
| m | 809 | Delft Blue |

| | | |
|---|---|---|
| ■ | 895 | Hunter Green, very dark |
| ⚠ | 3078 | Golden Yellow, very light |
| ∅ | 3345 | Hunter Green, dark |
| ★ | 3346 | Hunter Green |
| 3 | 3347 | Yellow Green, medium |
| ✗ | 3348 | Yellow Green, light |
| ◗ | 3756 | Baby Blue, ultra very light |

**Kreinik™ #4 Braid**

| | | |
|---|---|---|
| ▨ | 210 | Gold Dust |

## Backstitch Instructions

Flowers and lettering: DMC 797 Royal Blue.
Greenery: DMC 895 Hunter Green, very dark.
Border: Kreinik #4 Braid 210 Gold Dust.

# August Gladiolus

**DMC® 6-Strand Embroidery Floss**

| | | |
|---|---|---|
| ★ | 304 | Christmas Red, medium |
| = | 321 | Christmas Red |
| ↪ | 498 | Christmas Red, dark |
| ✖ | 666 | Christmas Red, bright |
| 3 | 772 | Yellow Green, very light |
| ☆ | 815 | Garnet, medium |
| ◢ | 816 | Garnet |
| ■ | 895 | Hunter Green, very dark |
| 4 | 3345 | Hunter Green, dark |
| ♥ | 3346 | Hunter Green |
| // | 3347 | Yellow Green, medium |
| ✗ | 3348 | Yellow Green, light |
| ➜ | 3705 | Melon, dark |
| 2 | 3706 | Melon, medium |
| :: | 3708 | Melon, light |
| ♡ | 3801 | Christmas Red, light |

**Kreinik™ #4 Braid**

| | | |
|---|---|---|
| ◨ | 210 | Gold Dust |

## Backstitch Instructions

Flowers: DMC 814 Garnet, dark.
Greenery and lettering: DMC 895 Hunter Green, very dark.
Border: Kreinik #4 Braid 210 Gold Dust.

## French Knot Instructions

• Lettering: DMC 895 Hunter Green, very dark.

©2002 Zweigart®

# September Aster

## DMC® 6-Strand Embroidery Floss

| | | | | | | |
|---|---|---|---|---|---|---|
| 3 | 319 | Pistachio Green, very dark | 2 | 743 | Yellow, medium | |
| ⌀ | 320 | Pistachio Green, medium | ✖ | 744 | Yellow, pale | |
| ■ | 333 | Blue Violet, very dark | // | 745 | Yellow, light pale | |
| ✗ | 340 | Blue Violet, medium | ♡ | 775 | Baby Blue, very light | |
| ↰ | 341 | Blue Violet, light | ✪ | 890 | Pistachio Green, ultra dark | |
| ➜ | 367 | Pistachio Green, dark | ☆ | 3746 | Blue Violet, dark | |
| ★ | 368 | Pistachio Green, light | ◗ | 3747 | Blue Violet, very light | |
| m | 369 | Pistachio Green, very light | ♥ | 3823 | Yellow, very pale | |
| ⌐ | 742 | Tangerine, light | **Kreinik™ #4 Braid** | | | |
| | | | ▨ | 210 | Gold Dust | |

## Backstitch Instructions

Flowers and lettering: DMC 333 Blue Violet, very dark.

Flower centers: DMC 742 Tangerine, light.

Greenery: DMC 890 Pistachio Green, ultra dark.

Border: Kreinik #4 Braid 210 Gold Dust.

# October Calendula

**DMC® 6-Strand Embroidery Floss**

| | | | | | | |
|---|---|---|---|---|---|---|
| ♡ | 433 | Brown, medium | m | 722 | Orange Spice, light |
| ⬤ | 434 | Brown, light | 2 | 745 | Yellow, light pale |
| Z | 435 | Brown, very light | ★ | 801 | Coffee Brown, dark |
| ➜ | 469 | Avocado Green | ■ | 920 | Copper, medium |
| // | 470 | Avocado Green, light | ◖ | 936 | Avocado Green, very dark |
| ✖ | 471 | Avocado Green, very light | 3 | 937 | Avocado Green, medium |
| ☆ | 472 | Avocado Green, ultra light | X | 3825 | Orange Spice, very light |
| ∩ | 720 | Orange Spice, dark | ⊘ | 3855 | Autumn Gold, light |
| ♥ | 721 | Orange Spice, medium | **Kreinik™ #4 Braid** | | |
| | | | ▨ | 210 | Gold Dust |

## Backstitch Instructions

Flowers and lettering: DMC 920 Copper, medium.

Greenery: DMC 936 Avocado Green, very dark.

Border: Kreinik #4 Braid 210 Gold Dust.

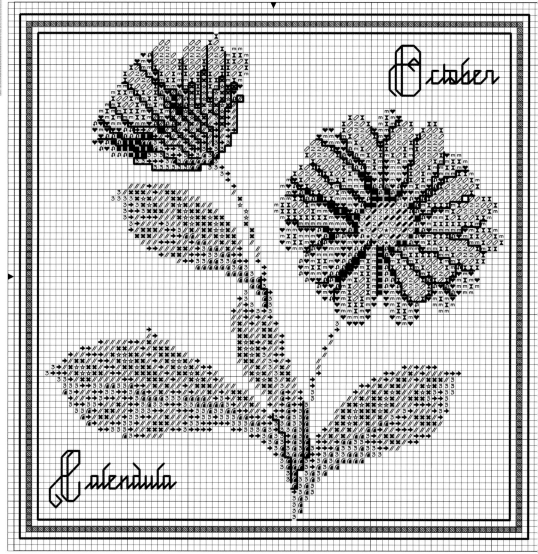

©2002 Zweigart®

# November Chrysanthemum

| DMC® 6-Strand Embroidery Floss | | | | | |
|---|---|---|---|---|---|
| = | 165 | Moss Green, very light | ★ | 3078 | Golden Yellow, very light |
| ✎ | 166 | Moss Green, medium light | ☆ | 3819 | Moss Green, light |
| ♥ | 580 | Moss Green, dark | ♡ | 3820 | Straw, dark |
| 2 | 581 | Moss Green | ✘ | 3821 | Straw |
| ◖ | 746 | Off White | m | 3822 | Straw, light |
| ⊘ | 782 | Topaz, dark | ♫ | 3823 | Yellow, very pale |
| ✗ | 783 | Topaz, medium | **Kreinik™ #4 Braid** | | |
| | | | ◩ | 210 | Gold Dust |

## Backstitch Instructions

Flower and lettering: DMC 781 Topaz, very dark.
Border: Kreinik #4 Braid 210 Gold Dust.

# December Poinsettia

**DMC® 6-Strand Embroidery Floss**

| | | | | | | |
|---|---|---|---|---|---|---|
| 2 | White | White | // | 3078 | Golden Yellow, very light |
| ♥ | 500 | Blue Green, very dark | ■ | 3328 | Salmon, dark |
| z | 501 | Blue Green, dark | ♡ | 3712 | Salmon, medium |
| ◪ | 502 | Blue Green | ✎ | 3713 | Salmon, very light |
| m | 503 | Blue Green, medium | ❽ | 3813 | Blue Green, light |
| 3 | 504 | Blue Green, light | ⌒ | 3820 | Straw, dark |
| ✗ | 760 | Salmon | ✖ | 3821 | Straw |
| ☆ | 761 | Salmon, light | 4 | 3822 | Straw, light |
| ★ | 783 | Topaz, medium | **Kreinik™ #4 Braid** | | |
| | | | ◩ | 210 | Gold Dust |

## Backstitch Instructions

Lettering and greenery: DMC 500 Blue Green, very dark.

Poinsettia center: DMC 782 Topaz, dark.

Poinsettia: DMC 3328 Salmon, dark.

Border: Kreinik #4 Braid 210 Gold Dust.

## French Knot Instructions

• Lettering: DMC 500 Blue Green, very dark.

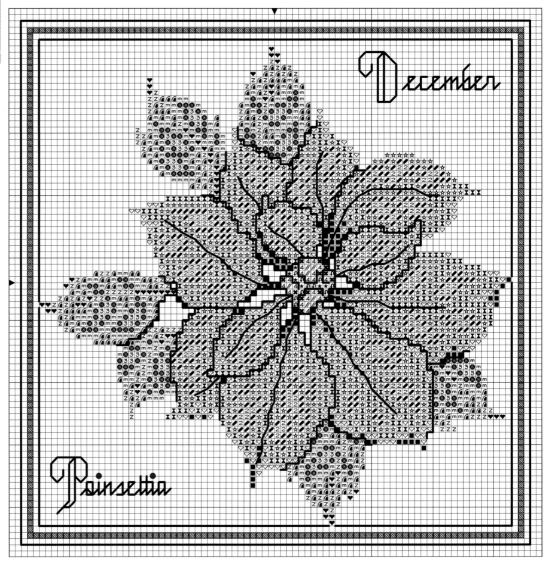

# Inspirational Wall Hanging

### *Design by Ursula Michael*

*The scripture verse of this beautiful piece reminds us to take time to appreciate and rejoice each day. That idea is further communicated by the brilliant shades of corals and greens that coordinate with the floral stitchband. Creative backstitch gives the appearance of intricate stitches, and the embellishments include red seed beads and a strawberry Glass Treasure.*

**Cross Stitch:** 2 strands
**Backstitch:** 1 strand
**French Knot:** 1 strand wrapped twice
**Stitch Counts:** 56 wide x 142 high
**Approximate Finished Size:**
    14-count fabric: 4" wide x 10⅛" high

**Supplies**
- 15" piece Zweigart® 14-Count Floral Stitchband #7425-19
- DMC® 6-Strand Embroidery Floss (1 skein each color)
- 1 package Mill Hill Red Seed Beads #02063
- Mill Hill Glass Treasure #12146 Red Strawberry
- 6"-wide Wall Hanger with Dowel
- #26 Tapestry Needle

## General Instructions

When cross stitch is complete, fold back the ends of the stitchband ½" and slipstitch, allowing room for a dowel at the top and bottom. Check size of dowel before slipstitching.

### DMC® 6-Strand Embroidery Floss

| | | |
|---|---|---|
| · | White | White |
| ✕ | 321 | Christmas Red |
| 5 | 350 | Coral, medium |
| ○ | 352 | Coral, light |
| ❖ | 726 | Topaz, light |
| ➜ | 816 | Garnet |
| ♥ | 3345 | Hunter Green, dark |
| ○ | 3347 | Yellow Green, medium |
| / | 3348 | Yellow Green, light |

## Backstitch Instructions

Band 1: DMC 816 Garnet.
Band 2, vines, and flowers: DMC 3347 Yellow Green, medium.
Band 3: DMC 321 Christmas Red.
Berries: DMC 902 Garnet, very dark.
Words: DMC 3345 Hunter Green, dark.

## French Knot Instructions

• Scripture: DMC 3345 Hunter Green, dark.

## Bead Instructions

• Attach Mill Hill red seed beads #02063 with DMC 350 Coral, medium. Refer to "Attaching a Bead" section in General Instructions, page 11, for further assistance, if necessary.

## Charm Instructions

Attach Mill Hill red Strawberry Glass Treasure #12146 with DMC 350 Coral, medium.

← Band 1
← Band 2
← Band 3

"This is the day the Lord has made

Let us rejoice and be glad"

Psalm 118:24

charm ← Band 3
← Band 2
← Band 1

# Poppy and Daisy Wreath Table Topper

**Design by Pam Kellogg**

*Add a dash of color to your home with these cheery poppies and daisies on a royal blue table topper. The prefinished table topper can be used alone as a centerpiece as we used it in the project photo, or as a topper over a solid colored tablecloth.*

**Cross Stitch:** 2 strands
**Backstitch:** 1 strand
**Stitch Counts:** 170 wide x 171 high
**Approximate Finished Size:**
   14-count fabric: 12⅛" wide x 12⅛" high

**Supplies**
- Zweigart® 14-Count Royal Blue Westerland Table Topper
- DMC® 6-Strand Embroidery Floss (1 skein each color)
- #24 Tapestry Needle

## DMC® 6-Strand Embroidery Floss

| Symbol | No. | Color | Symbol | No. | Color | Symbol | No. | Color |
|---|---|---|---|---|---|---|---|---|
| ◊ | | White White | ▣ | 666 | Christmas Red, bright | 3 | 898 | Coffee Brown, very dark |
| ⊘ | 321 | Christmas Red | ✖ | 712 | Cream | ◢ | 936 | Avocado Green, very dark |
| ⊙ | 433 | Brown, medium | 4 | 725 | Topaz | L | 937 | Avocado Green, medium |
| ▼ | 434 | Brown, light | Z | 738 | Tan, very light | ■ | 938 | Coffee Brown, ultra dark |
| ◤ | 435 | Brown, very light | △ | 739 | Tan, ultra very light | V | 3705 | Melon, dark |
| ? | 436 | Tan | // | 743 | Yellow, medium | / | 3706 | Melon, medium |
| ↑ | 437 | Tan, light | 2 | 744 | Yellow, pale | ● | 3708 | Melon, light |
| m | 469 | Avocado Green | ♡ | 745 | Yellow, light pale | ○ | 3801 | Christmas Red, light |
| ·|· | 470 | Avocado Green, light | ✚ | 776 | Pink, medium | ➜ | 3823 | Yellow, very pale |
| — | 471 | Avocado Green, very light | I | 801 | Coffee Brown, dark | ▲ | 3829 | Old Gold, very dark |
| # | 472 | Avocado Green, ultra light | ✗ | 818 | Baby Pink | 枀 | 3852 | Straw, very dark |
| ♥ | 498 | Christmas Red, dark | ‖ | 819 | Baby Pink, light | = | 3865 | Winter White |

## Backstitch Instructions

Small pink flowers: DMC 498 Christmas Red, dark.
All other backstitch: DMC 801 Coffee Brown, dark.

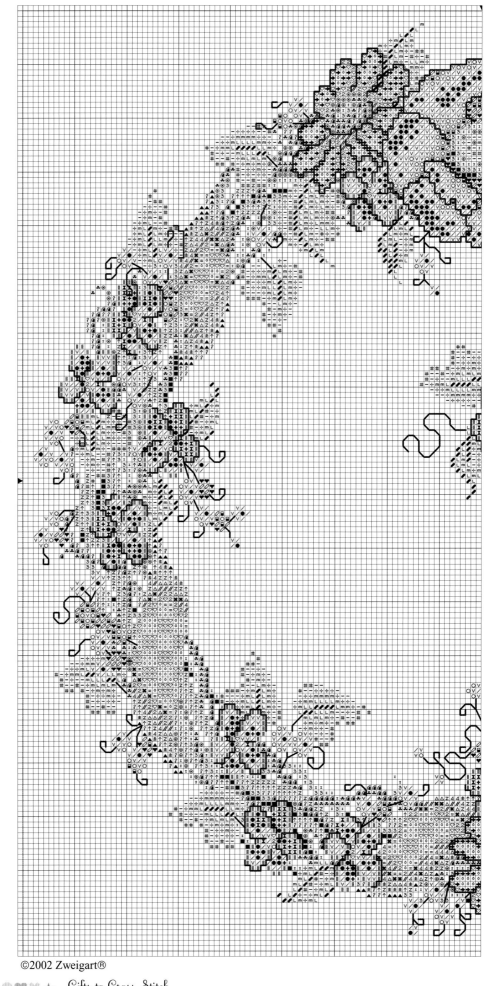

# Victorian Roses Jewelry Box and Table Topper

***Designs by Pam Kellogg***
***(floral on jewelry box and table topper)***

***and Lois Winston***
***(lettering on jewelry box)***

*Miniature Victorian roses adorn the beautiful "Stitched with Love for You" musical jewelry box. Accented with eyelet stitches and beads, this project will be a treasured gift from the heart.*

*An elegant table topper with coordinating Victorian roses accompanies this project.*

## Jewelry Box

**Cross Stitch:** 2 strands
**Backstitch:** 1 strand
**Stitch Count:**
 98 wide x 66 high
**Approximate Finished Size:**
 36-count fabric stitched over two threads =
 18-count fabric: 5⅜" wide x 3⅝" high

### Supplies
- Zweigart® 36-Count White Edinburgh Linen or 18-Count Fabric
- DMC® 6-Strand Embroidery Floss (1 skein each color)
- 1 package Mill Hill Petite Beads #40479
- 1 package Mill Hill Glass Seed Beads #02019
- Sudberry House Music Jewelry Box #99451
- DMC® 6-Strand Rayon Floss (1 skein each color)
- #26 Tapestry Needle
- Beading Needle

## General Instructions

This design has to be stitched on 36-count linen (over two threads) or on 18-count fabric (over one thread) in order for it to fit within the space on the jewelry box cover. Keycode is the same for both the jewelry box and table topper.

## Backstitch Instructions

Lettering: DMC 814 Garnet, dark.
Curlicues and stems: DMC 890 Pistachio Green, ultra dark.

## Eyelet Stitch Instructions

All eyelet stitches: DMC Rayon Floss B5200 White.

## Bead Instructions

• Beads within flowers: DMC 745 Pale Yellow to attach Mill Hill crystal honey seed beads #02019.
◦ Beads in eyelet stitches in border and around verse: DMC B5200 White to attach Mill Hill white petite beads #40479.
Refer to "Attaching a Bead" section in General Instructions, page 11, for further assistance, if necessary.

## DMC® 6-Strand Embroidery Floss

| | | | | | | | | |
|---|---|---|---|---|---|---|---|---|
| ■ | 150 | Pink, dark | ✖ | 368 | Pistachio Green, light | ◖ | 3747 | Blue Violet, very light |
| m | 151 | Pink | ☆ | 369 | Pistachio Green, very light | // | 3855 | Autumn Gold, light |
| 3 | 319 | Pistachio Green, very dark | ♥ | 890 | Pistachio Green, ultra dark | | | |
| ◔ | 320 | Pistachio Green, medium | 2 | 3350 | Dusty Rose, ultra dark | | | |
| ◐ | 340 | Blue Violet, medium | ◣ | 3354 | Dusty Rose, light | | | |
| 4 | 341 | Blue Violet, light | ✗ | 3731 | Dusty Rose, very dark | | | |
| → | 367 | Pistachio Green, dark | ♡ | 3733 | Dusty Rose | | | |

**Eyelet Stitches**
**DMC® 6-Strand Rayon Floss**
※　B5200 White

## Table Topper

**Cross Stitch:** 4 strands
**Backstitch:** 2 strands
**Stitch Count:** 87 wide x 87 high
**Approximate Finished Size:**
    10-count fabric:
    9⅝" wide x 9⅝" high

**Supplies**

- Beautiful Accents™ 10-Count White Prefinished Tula® Table Topper
- DMC® 6-Strand Embroidery Floss (2 skeins each color)
- #22 Tapestry Needle

# Victorian Roses Table Topper

## General Instructions

Leave eight to 10 rows between the beginning of the lace trim and where you start stitching. This design can be stitched in one corner if only the front of the topper will be shown, or in all four corners if the planned display calls for a symmetric treatment instead.

## Backstitch Instructions

All backstitch: DMC 890 Pistachio Green, ultra dark.

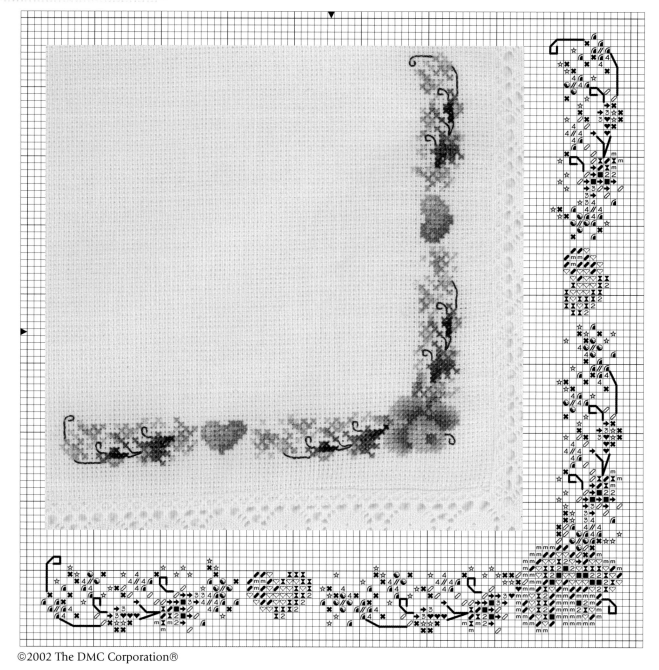

**Cross Stitch:** 2 strands
**Backstitch:** 1 strand
**Stitch Count:** 125 wide x 97 high (complete sampler)
**Approximate Finished Size:**
28-count fabric stitched over two threads = 14-count
14-count fabric: 9" wide x 7" high

**Supplies**
- 28-Count Fabric (stitched over two threads)
  or 14-Count fabric (for sampler)
- 14-count White Aida Coaster
- Beautiful Accents™ Plastic Checkbook Cover
- Wichelt 28-Count White Linen (stitched over two threads)
  or 14-Count Fabric (for checkbook cover)
- Beautiful Accents™ 10-Count
  White Damask Prefinished Purse
- Mouse Pad Kit
- White Sweatshirt
- Charles Craft 8.5-Count Waste Fabric (canvas)
- Anchor® 6-Strand Embroidery Floss (1 skein each color)
- Standard 7" x 9" Frame
- #24 Tapestry Needle

# Pink Rose Alphabet

### Designs by Roberta Madeleine

*Using the beautiful rose alphabet and your imagination, project ideas seem to open up just like a rose unfolds from a bud. Create personalized gifts that are usable: mouse pads, checkbook covers, key chains, coasters, towels, clothing, and more. And the real beauty of it: a single initial can be stitched in one hour!*

# Backstitch Instructions

Vines: Anchor 218 Juniper, dark.

## Anchor® 6-Strand Embroidery Floss

| | | | | | | |
|---|---|---|---|---|---|---|
| □ | 26 | Carnation, medium light | | ↓ | 54 | China Rose, dark |
| ▼ | 29 | Carnation, dark | | – | 55 | Beauty Rose, light |
| L | 35 | Blush, dark | | I | 211 | Spruce, medium dark |
| + | 48 | China Rose, very light | | ☆ | 226 | Emerald, medium light |
| ○ | 49 | China Rose, light | | ● | 240 | Grass Green, light |
| ◢ | 50 | China Rose, medium | | ■ | 1005 | Cherry Red, medium |
| ♡ | 52 | China Rose, medium dark | | ⊥ | 1038 | Glacier Blue, medium |

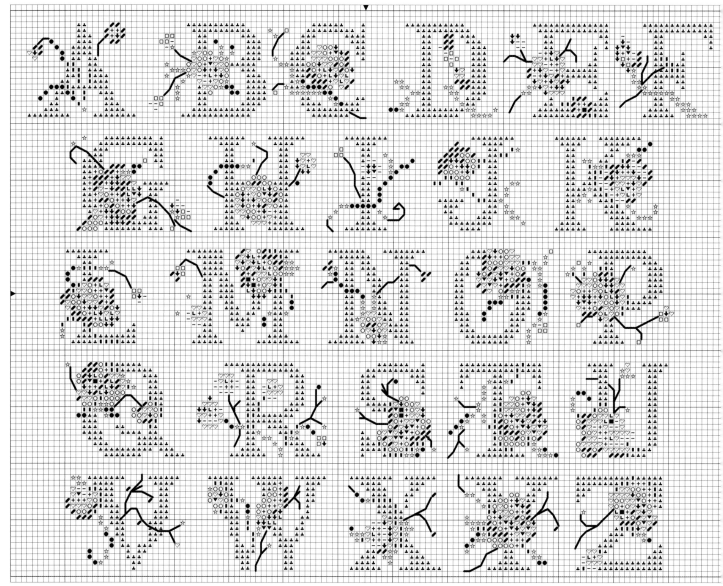

# Pink Roses Sweatshirt

Following manufacturer's instructions (or refer to page 10 of this book), use 8.5-count waste fabric (canvas) and stitch three initials centered on sweatshirt.

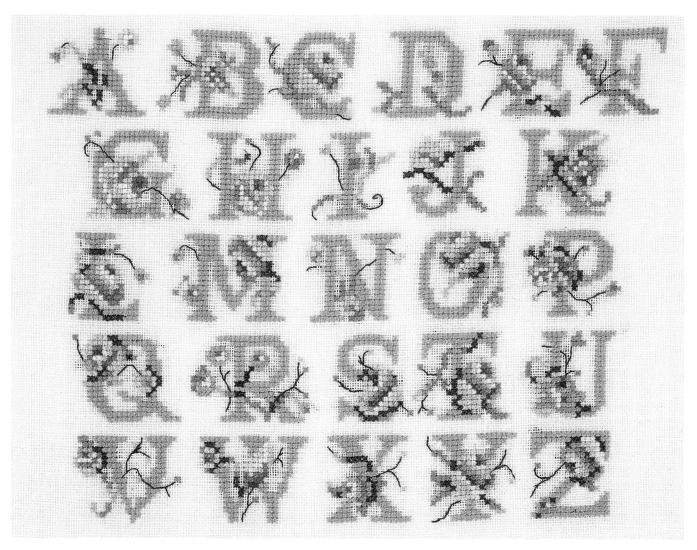

# Pink Roses Sampler

Stitch entire alphabet over two threads on 28-count fabric or over one thread on 14-count fabric.
The finished sampler fits within a standard frame with 7" x 9" opening.

# Pink Roses Checkbook Cover

Stitch three initials over two threads on 28-count fabric or over one thread on 14-count fabric. Follow manufacturer's instructions for mounting in plastic checkbook cover.

# Pink Roses Damask Purse

Using three strands of floss, stitch one initial on 10-count white damask purse.

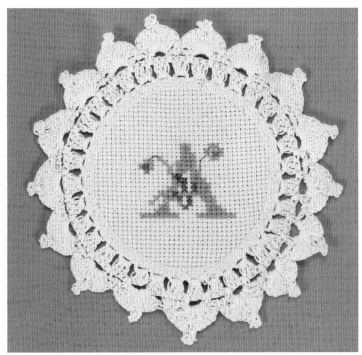

# Pink Roses Coaster

Stitch one initial on white 14-count coaster.

# Pink Roses Mouse Pad

Stitch one initial in lower left corner of 14-count white Aida for mouse pad kit. Follow manufacturer's instructions for mounting on mouse pad.

# Gifts for Mother's Day

**Cross Stitch:** 2 strands
**Backstitch:** 2 strands
**Stitch Counts:** 23 wide x 91 high
**Approximate Finished Size:**
   14-count fabric: 1⅝" wide x 6½"
   high (each flower motif)

**Supplies**
- Zweigart® 14-Count White Stitchband #7324-1
- Anchor® 6-Strand Embroidery Floss (1 skein each color)
- #24 Tapestry Needle
- Scissors
- Iron

# General Instructions

Center design on stitchband.

When cross stitch is completed, press stitchband with iron and then trim excess fabric at both ends of bookmark.

Finish bookmark by folding ¼" at each end and slipstitching on back of bookmark.

**Anchor® 6-Strand Embroidery Floss**

| | | |
|---|---|---|
| ↑ | 19 | Burgundy, medium |
| I | 31 | Blush, light |
| ✕ | 35 | Blush, dark |
| V | 243 | Grass Green, medium |
| ◣ | 246 | Grass Green, very dark |

# Backstitch Instructions

Vines and "Mother": Anchor 243 Grass Green, medium.

# Mother Bookmark

### Design by Ursula Michael

*A special bookmark for a special mother! This is a really quick-to-stitch project. In fact, you can complete it in one night. When it is finished, present the gift in a birthday, Christmas, or Mother's Day card...or in one of your mother's favorite books. She is sure to appreciate this thoughtful sentiment.*

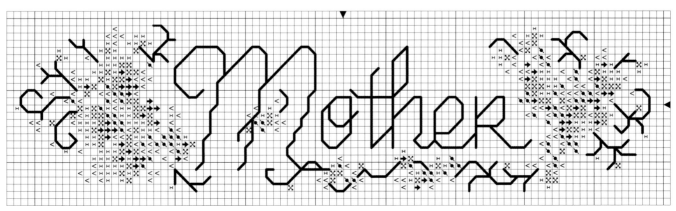

©2002 Zweigart®

**Cross Stitch:** 2 strands
**Backstitch:** 1 strand
**French Knot:** 1 strand wrapped twice
**Stitch Counts:** 54 wide x 54 high
**Approximate Finished Size:**
32-count fabric <u>stitched over two threads</u> = 16 count
16-count fabric: 3⅜" wide x 3⅜" high

**Supplies**
- Wichelt 32-Count Ivory Linen or 16-Count Fabric
- Anchor® 6-Strand Embroidery Floss (1 skein each color)
- 1 spool Kreinik™ High Luster Blending Filament
- Anne Brinkley CT 4 Lead Crystal Jar
- #24 Tapestry Needle

# Mom's Crystal Jar

### Design by Roberta Madeleine

*A personalized "Mom" crystal jar will capture any mother's heart. It's a gift guaranteed to be treasured and displayed for years.*

*Fill the crystal jar with mom's favorite potpourri or let her decide what to put in it. Either way, it's a gift mothers will enjoy.*

# General Instructions

This project was stitched over two threads on 32-count linen in order to fit within the jar opening. An alternate fabric would be 16-count Aida.

When stitching with a blended needle, use one strand of floss and one strand of blending filament.

## Anchor® 6-Strand Embroidery Floss

| | | | | | | |
|---|---|---|---|---|---|---|
| □ | 27 | Carnation, medium | | ■ | 240 | Grass Green, light |
| ▼ | 46 | Crimson Red | | ◣ | 241 | Grass Green |
| ✚ | 54 | China Rose, dark | | 2 | 288 | Canary Yellow, light |
| ☆ | 140 | Copen Blue, light | | ♡ | 305 | Topaz, light |
| C | 142 | Copen Blue, medium | | ○ | 887 | Sandstone, medium light |
| I | 161 | Sapphire, medium | | △ | 906 | Brass, dark |
| ↑ | 203 | Mint Green, light | | | | |
| ● | 205 | Mint Green, dark | | | | |
| L | 206 | Spruce, light | | | | |
| ⊥ | 208 | Spruce, medium light | | | | |

### Blended Needle

╱  Anchor 941 Stormy Blue, very dark <u>and</u>
Kreinik™ High Luster Blending Filament 051 Sapphire

## Backstitch Instructions

Pink flowers: Anchor 54 China Rose, dark.
Blue flowers: Anchor 142 Copen Blue, medium.
Vines and stems: Anchor 205 Mint Green, dark.

## French Knot Instructions

● Placement indicated on chart: Anchor 54 China Rose, dark.

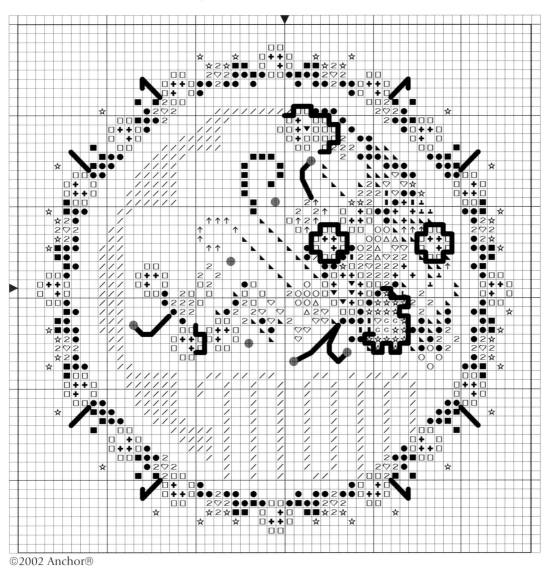

©2002 Anchor®

# Rose Shawl

**Design by Roberta Madeleine**

*Luxurious in Victorian rose motifs and softness, this shawl is sure to be an instant favorite. It's a great gift for mothers, grandmothers, aunts, friends—and even for yourself! The lightweight fabric is perfect for those chilly spring-summer evenings.*

*Stitching this 7-count Country Aida prefinished shawl is easy on the eyes and very quick to stitch and only requires fringing for finishing. This shawl was completed in less than one week.*

## General Instructions

Read these instructions carefully before stitching so that motifs fit properly on the shawl.

Stitch large rose motif centered on shawl, approximately 9" down from the top of the shawl as model is shown. Be sure to leave at least 22 spaces between the large rose motif and where the single motifs start. Or, stitch large rose motif starting at the top of the shawl.

Stitch single motifs starting four spaces from the basting hem of the shawl, leaving 22 spaces from the large rose motif (unless you stitched the large rose motif at the top of the shawl).

Leave one space between each of the single motifs that go along the two bottom edges.

## Floss Instructions

If stitching with 6-strand embroidery floss in place of the #3 pearl cotton, use four strands of floss for cross stitch and two strands for backstitch. The color numbers would be the same for the embroidery floss as shown in the keycode for the pearl cotton.

## Backstitch Instructions

Rose: DMC 321 Christmas Red.
Leaves: DMC 3345 Hunter Green, dark.

| | DMC® #3 Pearl Cotton | |
|---|---|---|
| : | White | White |
| ▼ | 321 | Christmas Red |
| L | 349 | Coral, dark |
| ➜ | 356 | Terra Cotta, medium |
| ■ | 498 | Christmas Red, light |
| V | 605 | Cranberry, very light |
| ★ | 776 | Pink, medium |
| = | 818 | Baby Pink |
| □ | 819 | Baby Pink, light |
| / | 951 | Terra Cotta, light |
| ♥ | 956 | Geranium |
| ✖ | 957 | Geranium, pale |
| 2 | 963 | Dusty Rose, ultra very light |
| ◢ | 987 | Forest Green, dark |
| Z | 989 | Forest Green |
| ⊥ | 3078 | Golden Yellow, very light |
| ● | 3345 | Hunter Green, dark |
| ♡ | 3348 | Yellow Green, light |

**Cross Stitch:** 1 strand
(#3 pearl cotton)
**Backstitch:** 1 strand
**Stitch Counts:** 98 wide x 99 high
(large rose motif)
19 wide x 21 high (single small motif)
**Approximate Finished Size:**
7-count fabric: 14" wide x 14⅛" high (large rose motif)
7-count fabric: 2¾" wide x 3" high (single small motif)

**Supplies**
- Beautiful Accents™ 7-Count Black Country Aida Prefinished Shawl
- DMC® #3 Pearl Cotton or 6-Strand Embroidery Floss
  - 1 skein each #321, #349, #356, #498, #605, #776, #818, #819, #951, #956, #957, #987, #989, #3078, and #3345
  - 3 skeins #963
  - 4 skeins #3348
- #20 Tapestry Needle

**Note:** Before you begin stitching, refer to the photos on the facing page as well as the layout diagram below for clarity on design placement. Notice how the large rose motif is pointing downward on the shawl.

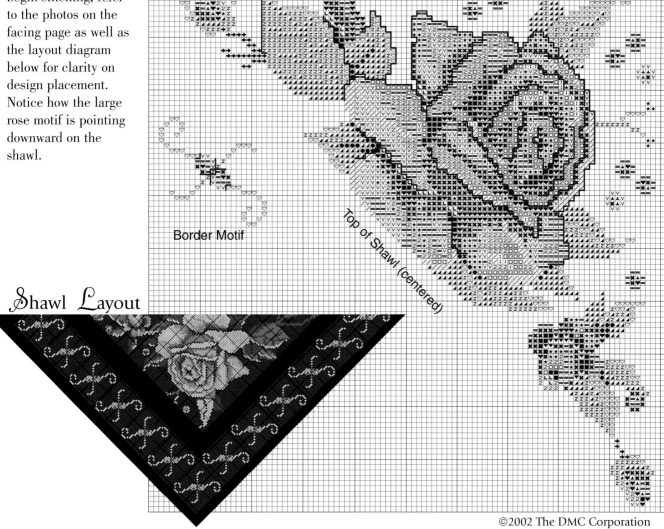

Border Motif

Top of Shawl (centered)

𝒮hawl ℒayout

# Gifts with Patriotic Flair

◆ ✎ ◐ ♥ ✕ ★  *Gifts to Cross Stitch*

# United We Stand Afghan and Pillow

### Design by Lois Winston

*Immediately following September 11, 2001, Zweigart Fabrics made a special patriotic fabric. All proceeds from the sale of the patriotic fabric still go to three charities: New York World Trade Center Relief Fund, American Red Cross, and The National Organization for Victim Assistance.*

*Designer Lois Winston, who lives only 18 miles from Ground Zero, graciously donated the designs for the Patriotic Afghan and Pillow Set.*

**Cross Stitch:** 4 strands
**Backstitch:** 2 strands
**Stitch Counts:** 37 wide x 29 high (United We Stand)
    39 wide x 39 high (heart)
    37 wide x 38 high (star)
**Approximate Finished Size:**
    18-count fabric stitched over two threads = 9-count
    9-count fabric: 4" wide x 4" high

**Supplies**
- Zweigart® 18-Count White Patriotic Afghan
- Zweigart® 18-Count White Patriotic Prefinished Ruffled Pillow Sham
- DMC® 6-Strand Embroidery Floss (1 skein each color)
- #26 Tapestry Needle

## General Instructions

The afghan and pillow sham projects were stitched over two threads.

## Afghan

Refer to diagram of layout for the placement of motifs.

When stitching the hearts, turn chart one-quarter turn so that each group of four hearts has bottoms pointing to center of group.

When stitching is complete, fringe.

## Pillow Sham

Stitch one star flag motif in center of pillow sham over two threads.

## Backstitch Instructions

All backstitch: DMC 823 Navy Blue, dark.

### DMC® 6-Strand Embroidery Floss

| | | |
|---|---|---|
| # | 666 | Christmas Red, light |
| ○ | 798 | Delft Blue, dark |
| ✕ | 820 | Royal Blue, very dark |
| ■ | 823 | Navy Blue, dark |
| • | B5200 | Snow White |

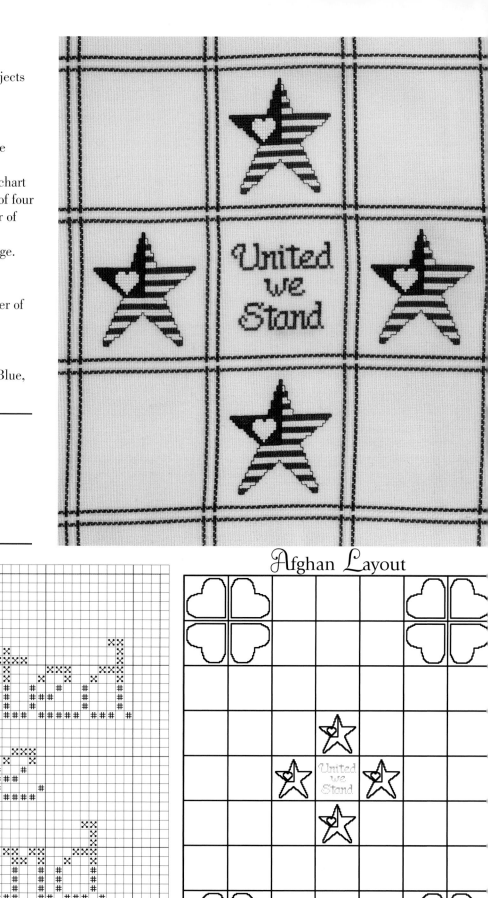

Afghan Layout

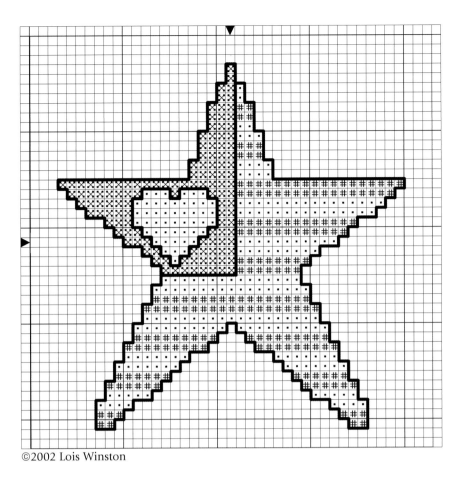

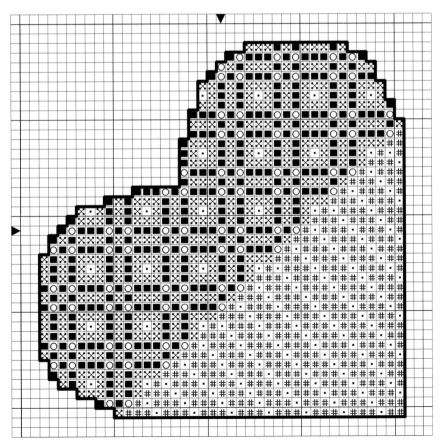

**Cross Stitch:** 2 strands
**Backstitch:** 1 strand (except "God Bless America", 2 strands)
**Stitch Counts:** 59 wide x 86 high
**Approximate Finished Size:**
    18-count fabric: 3¼" wide x 4¾" high

**Supplies**
- Daniel Enterprises Custom Single Switchplate Cover
- Crafter's Pride 18-Count Vinyl Weave
- DMC® 6-Strand Embroidery Floss
    (1 skein each color)
- #24 Tapestry Needle

# God Bless America Switchplate

### Design by Laura Doyle

*Add pizzazz to your décor with a customized stitched switchplate. Stitch the patriotic bear to commemorate your true American pride.*

## General Instructions

This project has to be stitched on 18-count fabric/vinyl weave in order for the design to fit within the switchplate cover.

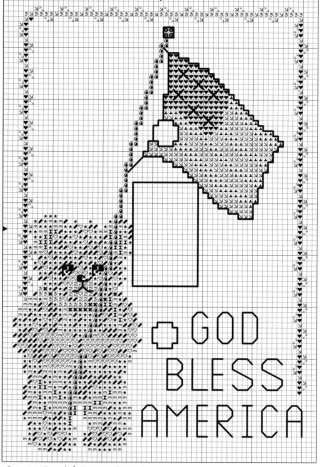

### DMC® 6-Strand Embroidery Floss

| Symbol | Number | Color |
|---|---|---|
| ■ | 310 | Black |
| 8 | 318 | Steel Gray, light |
| ↙ | 321 | Christmas Red |
| ◖ | 414 | Steel Gray, dark |
| m | 610 | Drab Brown, dark |
| ★ | 611 | Drab Brown |
| ✎ | 612 | Drab Brown, light |
| ♡ | 613 | Drab Brown, very light |
| ♥ | 797 | Royal Blue |
| 3 | 798 | Delft Blue, dark |
| ✖ | 799 | Delft Blue, medium |
| 2 | 822 | Beige Gray, light |
| ✖ | 3021 | Brown Gray, very dark |
| ⊥ | B5200 | Snow White |

## Backstitch Instructions

Mouth and eyes: DMC 310 Black.
Around flag: DMC 318 Steel Gray, light.
Top of flagpole: DMC 414 Steel Gray, dark.
"God Bless America": two strands DMC 798 Delft Blue, dark.
Stars on flag: DMC B5200 Snow White.

# Proud To Be An American Mouse Pad

### Design by Pam Kellogg

*After September 11, 2001, Americans became even more proud of America and for what America stands for. Flags are seen more frequently in yards, stores, and even on cars. This "Proud To Be An American" mouse pad is a quick and inexpensive gift that any proud American would be pleased to display at an office or home computer. As with many designs, it could also be stitched on a sweatshirt.*

**Cross Stitch:** 2 strands
**Backstitch:** 1 strand
**Stitch Counts:** 95 wide x 81 high
**Approximate Finished Size:**
   14-count fabric: 6¾" wide x 5¾" high

**Supplies**
- Beautiful Accents™ Mouse Pad Kit with 14-Count White Aida Fabric
- DMC® 6-Strand Embroidery Floss (1 skein each color)
- #24 Tapestry Needle

# General Instructions

When cross stitch is completed, follow manufacturer's instructions for mounting Aida fabric to mouse pad.

# Backstitch Instructions

Wording: DMC 823 Navy Blue, dark.

## DMC® 6-Strand Embroidery Floss

| | | | | | | |
|---|---|---|---|---|---|---|
| m | 304 | Christmas Red, medium | ↘ | 666 | Christmas Red, bright |
| ( | 311 | Navy Blue, medium | ✗ | 815 | Garnet, medium |
| :: | 312 | Navy Blue, light | 4 | 816 | Garnet |
| ⊖ | 321 | Christmas Red | ■ | 823 | Navy Blue, dark |
| ✗ | 322 | Navy Blue, very light | 2 | 3325 | Baby Blue, light |
| // | 334 | Baby Blue, medium | ♡ | 3705 | Melon, dark |
| ↶ | 336 | Navy Blue | ♥ | 3755 | Baby Blue |
| ◢ | 498 | Christmas Red, dark | ◮ | 3801 | Christmas Red, light |

# Patriotic Flag Ornaments

**Designs by Ursula Michael**

*Why not make it a patriotic Christmas with these heart, square, and bell-shaped ornaments? They make a great gift set to be cherished for years to come.*

*Another idea for the patriotic flag designs is to stitch them as one group and then mat and frame them for enjoyment throughout the year.*

**Cross Stitch:** 2 strands
**Stitch Counts:** 60 wide x 134 high (complete group)
  60 wide x 37 high (heart)
  40 wide x 40 high (square)
  50 wide x 53 high (bell)
**Approximate Finished Sizes:**
  18-count fabric: 3⅛" wide x 7½" high (complete group)
  18-count fabric: 3⅛" wide x 2⅛" high (heart)
  18-count fabric: 2¼" wide x 2¼" high (square)
  18-count fabric: 2¾" wide x 3" high (bell)

**Supplies**
- 3 pieces 5"-Square 18-Count Antique White Aida Fabric (for ornaments)
- 6" x 10" piece 18-count Antique White Aida Fabric (for framed picture, optional)
- Anchor® 6-Strand Embroidery Floss (1 skein each color)
- ½-yard ¼" Cording (per ornament)
- #24 Tapestry Needle
- Sweet Suspension Frames: Bell, Heart, and Square (optional)

## General Instructions

When cross stitch is completed, follow manufacturer's instructions for mounting.

**Anchor® 6-Strand Embroidery Floss**

| | | |
|---|---|---|
| — | White | White |
| ✕ | 133 | Royal Blue, dark |
| ● | 9046 | Christmas Red |

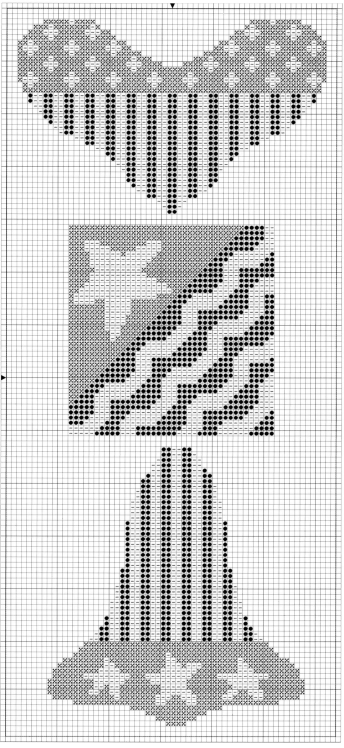

©2002 Anchor®

# Gifts for
# Special Events

# Reach for the Stars Graduation Frame

**Design by Ursula Michael**

*Capture a graduate's special moment in time with a unique frame. Star and rainbow motifs surround the inspiring message, "Reach For The Stars." The graduation year is displayed within the design. With no backstitching in this project, the stitching goes very quickly! The project is appropriate for male and female graduates. The acrylic frame comes with a precut 18-count white vinyl weave insert for stitching. When the stitching is complete, simply place in frame along with graduate's picture.*

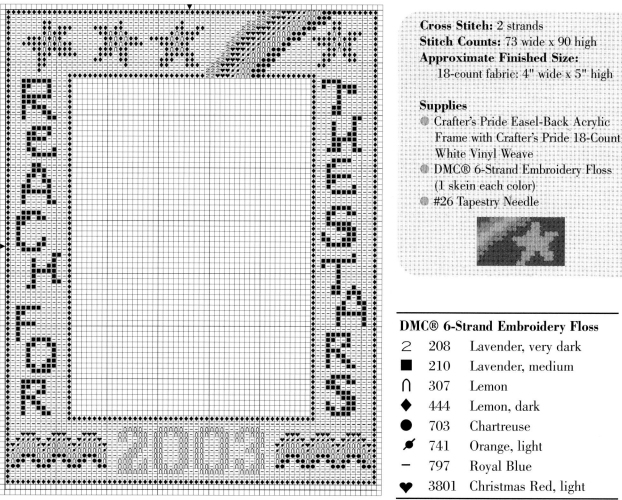

**Cross Stitch:** 2 strands
**Stitch Counts:** 73 wide x 90 high
**Approximate Finished Size:**
   18-count fabric: 4" wide x 5" high

**Supplies**
- Crafter's Pride Easel-Back Acrylic Frame with Crafter's Pride 18-Count White Vinyl Weave
- DMC® 6-Strand Embroidery Floss (1 skein each color)
- #26 Tapestry Needle

### DMC® 6-Strand Embroidery Floss

| Symbol | No. | Color |
|---|---|---|
| 2 | 208 | Lavender, very dark |
| ■ | 210 | Lavender, medium |
| ∩ | 307 | Lemon |
| ◆ | 444 | Lemon, dark |
| ● | 703 | Chartreuse |
| ✎ | 741 | Orange, light |
| − | 797 | Royal Blue |
| ♥ | 3801 | Christmas Red, light |

©2002 Daniel Enterprises

# Bar Mitzvah Sampler

### Design by Lois Winston

*In Hebrew, bar mitzvah means "son of the commandment" or "servant of the commandment." It is a Jewish religious ceremony and celebration marking the formal entry into adulthood of boys at age 13. At that time, a boy is deemed qualified to be counted a part of a minyan (the quorum of 10 men meeting for public prayer) and can began wearing teffin (phylacteries), small square leather boxes containing slips inscribed with scripture passages. Orthodox men during weekday-morning prayers wear these on the left arm and forehead.*

*There is reading from the Torah to honor the bar mitzvah's new status as a full-fledged member of the religious community. This is followed with a festive meal and this sampler would be an appropriate gift to celebrate this rite of passage.*

**Cross Stitch:** 2 strands (floss);
 2 strands (metallic floss)
**Backstitch:** 1 strand
**Stitch Counts:** 106 wide x 76 high
**Approximate Finished Size:**
 25-count fabric <u>stitched over</u>
 <u>two threads</u> = 12½-count
 12½-count fabric: 8½" wide x 6" high

**Supplies**
- DMC® 25-Count Winter White Evenweave #3865
- DMC® 6-Strand Embroidery Floss (1 skein each color)
- 10" x 13" Frame
- #26 Tapestry Needle

## General Instructions

This design was stitched over two threads on 25-count fabric to fit into a standard 10" x 13" frame.

## Backstitch Instructions

Name and words: DMC 311 Navy Blue, medium.
All other backstitch: DMC 310 Black.

### DMC® 6-Strand Embroidery Floss

| | | | | | | | | | |
|---|---|---|---|---|---|---|---|---|---|
| ✕ | 322 | Navy Blue, very light | Ƨ | 437 | Tan, light | / | 3325 | Baby Blue, light |
| ○ | 334 | Baby Blue, medium | · | 747 | Sky Blue, very light | ● | 3765 | Peacock Blue, very dark |
| ■ | 433 | Brown, medium | ♡ | 806 | Peacock Blue, dark | \ | 3766 | Peacock Blue, light |
| △ | 435 | Brown, very light | + | 807 | Peacock Blue | — | 3841 | Baby Blue, pale |

### DMC® 6-Strand Metallic Floss

| | | | | | |
|---|---|---|---|---|---|
| ♥ | 5282 | Gold | ★ | 5284 | Gold, dark |

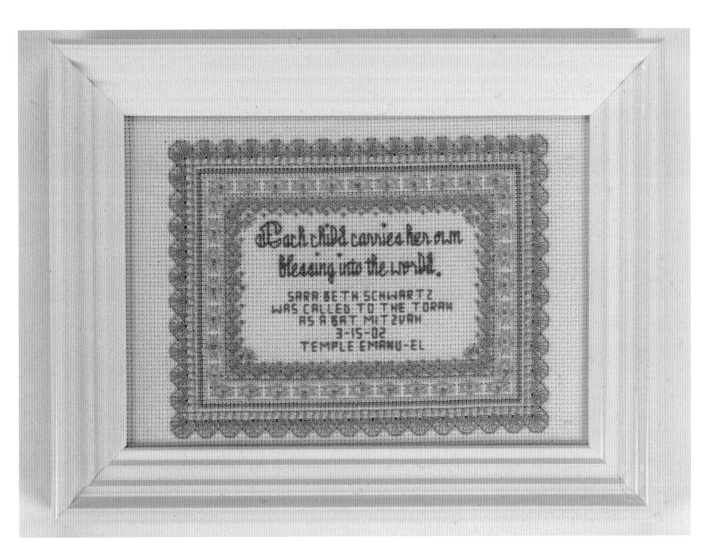

# Bat Mitzvah Sampler

### *Design by Lois Winston*

*In Hebrew, bat mitzvah means "daughter of the commandment" or "servant of the commandment." It is a Jewish religious ceremony and celebration marking the formal entry into adulthood of girls at age 12.*

*Jewish women were not called to the Torah until the advent of Reform Judaism in the 19th century. Rabbi Mordecai Kaplan started the bat mitzvah early in the 20th century for his daughter in 1922. Orthodox Jews still do not hold bat mitzvah ceremonies.*

*Ceremony preparations usually begin a year or more in advance, which is more than ample time to stitch this beautiful sampler to commemorate the grand event, presenting it to the young woman at the party held after the ceremony.*

**Cross Stitch:** 1 strand pearl cotton
**Long Stitch:** 1 strand pearl cotton
**Backstitch:** 1 strand (pearl cotton)
**Stitch Counts:** 96 wide x 72 high
**Approximate Finished Size:**
    18-count fabric: 5⅜" wide x 4" high

**Supplies**
- DMC® 18-Count Light Sea Green Aida #964
- DMC® #12 Pearl Cotton (1 skein each color)
- 5" x 7" Frame
- #24 Tapestry Needle

## DMC #12 Pearl Cotton

O    503     Blue Green, medium

·     3753    Antique Blue, ultra very light

## Long Stitch Instructions

    Inner and outer lace borders: DMC 3042 Antique Violet, light.

    Jewish stars: DMC 932 Antique Blue, light.

## French Knot Instructions

- Within outer border: DMC 225 Shell Pink, ultra very light.
- Within Jewish stars: DMC 932 Antique Blue, light.
- Around inner border: DMC 503 Blue Green, medium.
- Verse: DMC 931 Antique Blue, medium.

## Backstitch Instructions

    "Each child…" verse: DMC 931 Antique Blue, medium.

    Name, date, "was called…," and place: DMC 223 Shell Pink, light.

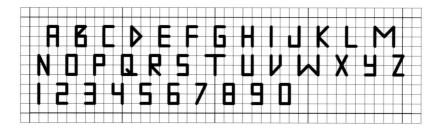

# Hanukkah/ Dreidel Song Sampler

**Design by Lois Winston**

Hanukkah or Chanukah (Hebrew for "dedication") is an annual Jewish festival celebrated on eight consecutive days. The festival begins on the 25th day of Kislev, the third month of the Jewish calendar. Hanukkah is also known as the Festival of Lights, Feast of Dedication, and Feast of the Maccabees.

The main feature of Hanukkah celebrations is the lighting of candles: one the first night, two the second, and so on until eight candles have been lit in a special candelabrum called a menorah. A blessing is said each night as the Hanukkah candles are lit.

Hanukkah is a festive family occasion with special foods and songs. Children sometimes play games with a spinning top called a dreidel during the eight days of the festival. This sampler captures that festive spirit by featuring the dreidel and its light-hearted verse.

**Cross Stitch:** 1 strand pearl cotton
**Backstitch:** 1 strand pearl cotton (stars); 1 strand floss (words and dreidels)
**Stitch Counts:** 76 wide x 90 high
**Approximate Finished Size:** 25-count fabric stitched over two threads = 12½-count
   12½-count fabric: 6" wide x 7¼" high

**Supplies**
- 10" x 12" Piece DMC® 25-Count Winter White Evenweave #3865
- DMC® #8 Pearl Cotton (1 skein each color)
- DMC® 6-Strand Embroidery Floss (1 skein each color)
- 8" x 10" Frame
- #24 Tapestry Needle

## General Instructions

This design was stitched over two threads on 25-count fabric to fit into a standard 8" x 10" frame.

## Backstitch Instructions

Jewish stars: DMC #8 Pearl Cotton 742 Tangerine, light.
Verse: DMC 6-Strand Embroidery Floss 820 Royal Blue, very dark.
Dreidels: DMC 6-Strand Embroidery Floss 310 Black.

## French Knot Instructions

• Verse: DMC 6-Strand Embroidery Floss 820 Royal Blue, very dark.

**DMC® #8 Pearl Cotton**

| | | | | | | | | | |
|---|---|---|---|---|---|---|---|---|---|
| ● | 208 | Lavender, very dark | ○ | 471 | Avocado Green, very light | / | 993 | Aquamarine, light |
| ■ | 340 | Blue Violet, medium | ✕ | 718 | Plum | ♥ | 995 | Electric Blue, dark |
| — | 352 | Coral, light | ▲ | 797 | Royal Blue | + | 3328 | Salmon, dark |

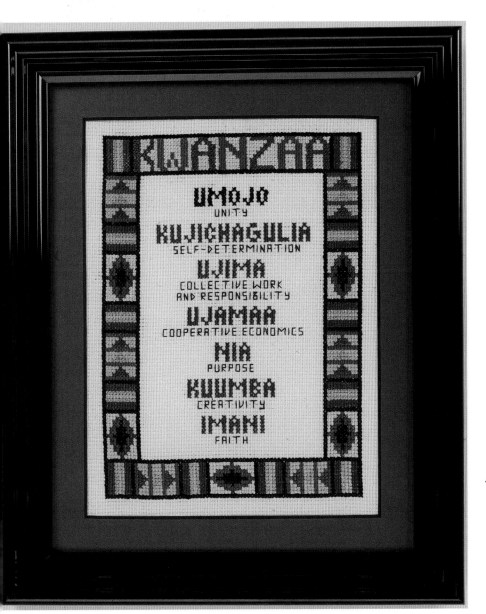

# Kwanzaa Sampler

**Design by Lois Winston**

The Organization Us is the founding organization of Kwanzaa with Dr. Maulana Karenga as the creator of the day of commemoration.

The seven candles of Kwanzaa represent the seven cultural principles of the African-American celebration: unity, self-determination, collective work and responsibility, cooperative economics, purpose, creativity, and faith.

The colors of Kwanzaa —black, red, and green— are stitched within this piece to help express the pride in the African heritage.

**Cross Stitch:** 2 strands (rayon floss)
**Backstitch:** 1 strand (embroidery floss)
**Stitch Counts:** 75 wide x 101 high
**Approximate Finished Size:**
   14-count fabric: 5⅜" wide x 7¼" high

**Supplies**
- 10" x 12" Piece DMC® 14-Count White Aida
- DMC® 6-Strand Rayon Floss (1 skein each color)
- DMC® 6-Strand Embroidery Floss (1 skein each color)
- 8" x 10" Frame
- #24 Tapestry Needle

## DMC® 6-Strand Rayon Floss

| | | | |
|---|---|---|---|
| . | 30307 | Lemon | (307) |
| ■ | 30310 | Black | (310) |
| ♡ | 30349 | Coral, dark | (349) |
| / | 30471 | Avocado Green, very light | (471) |
| ✕ | 30606 | Orange-Red, bright | (606) |
| ● | 30700 | Christmas Green, bright | (700) |
| – | 30972 | Canary, Deep | (972) |

Note: The numbers in parenthesis indicate the embroidery floss substitution.

## Backstitch Instructions
   Verse: DMC 6-Strand Embroidery Floss 310 Black.

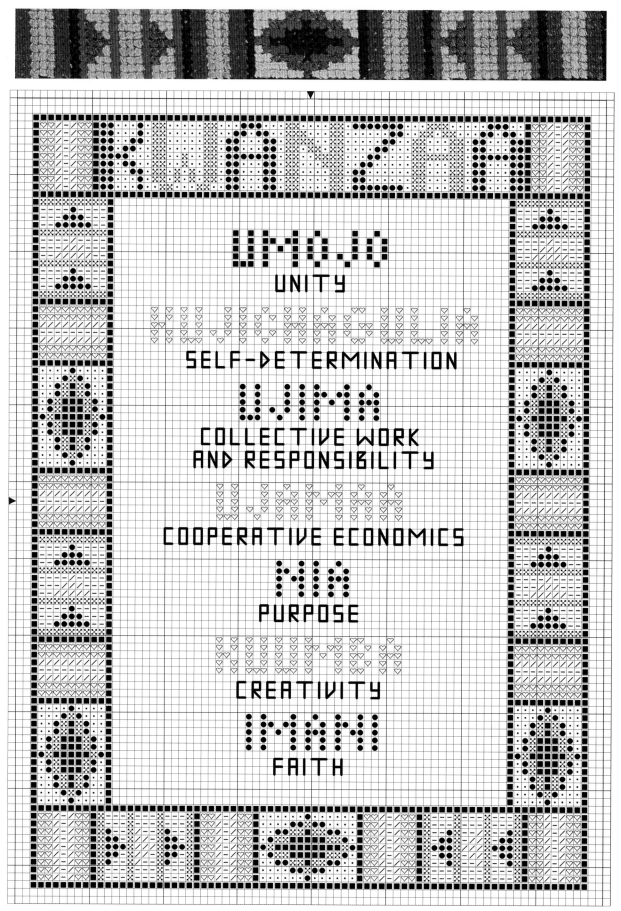

UMOJA
UNITY

SELF-DETERMINATION

UJIMA
COLLECTIVE WORK
AND RESPONSIBILITY

COOPERATIVE ECONOMICS

NIA
PURPOSE

CREATIVITY

IMANI
FAITH

# Gifts for
# Weddings

# Wedding Album Cover

### Design by Roberta Madeleine

*This album cover is strikingly beautiful with its unique theme of shades of turquoise. It's embellished with sparkling glass beads and high-luster blending filament to give it even more sparkle.*

*This album cover is prefinished, so all that is required is cross stitch on the cover and it fits any standard size three-ring binder with a 1½" spine.*

**Cross Stitch:** 2 strands
**Backstitch:** 1 strand
**Stitch Counts:** 76 wide x 110 high
**Approximate Finished Size:**
   14-count fabric: 5½" wide x 7⅞" high

**Supplies**
- Beautiful Accents™ 14-Count White Aida Prefinished Album Cover
- Anchor® 6-Strand Embroidery Floss (1 skein each color)
- 1 spool Kreinik™ High Luster Blending Filament
- 1 package Mill Hill Robin Egg Blue Seed Beads #00143
- #24 Tapestry Needle
- Beading Needle

**Blended Needle (1 strand of each)**

☐    Anchor® 6-Strand Embroidery Floss 928 Sky Blue, light,
<u>and</u> Kreinik™ High Luster Blending Filament 014HL Sky Blue, light

## Backstitch Instructions

All backstitch: Anchor 1039 Wedgwood, light.

## French Knot Instructions

• Names: Anchor 1039 Wedgwood, light.

## Bead Instructions

• Attach Mill Hill seed beads with Anchor 928 Sky Blue, light. Refer to "Attaching a Bead" section in General Instructions, page 11, for further assistance, if necessary.

©2002 Anchor®

# Ring Bearer's Pillow

### Design by Phyllis Dobbs

*This luxurious damask ring bearer's pillow will be a delightful addition to any wedding service. White-on-white with embellishments of pearls and a fluted crystal heart make this a cherished keepsake of the couple's special day.*

*And to help alleviate any additional pre-wedding stress, the prefinished pillow has a 10-count fabric center area for quick and easy stitching.*

**Cross Stitch:** 1 strand (pearl cotton #5)
or 3 strands embroidery floss
**Backstitch:** 1 strand
**Stitch Counts:** 34 wide x 34 high
**Approximate Finished Size:**
10-count fabric: 3⅜" wide x 3⅜" high

**Supplies**
- Beautiful Accents™ 10-Count White Damask Prefinished Ring Bearer's Pillow
- DMC® #5 Pearl Cotton (1 skein each color)
- DMC® 6-Strand Metallic Floss (1 skein each color)
- 21 2.5mm Pearl Beads
- Mill Hill Fluted Heart Glass Treasure #12208
- #22 Tapestry Needle

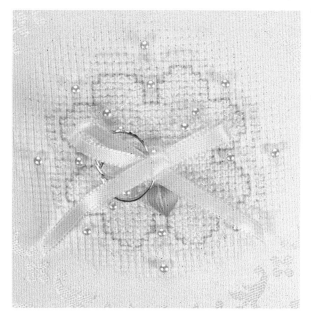

**DMC® 6-Strand Metallic Floss**
✕  5272  White
**DMC®#5 Pearl Cotton**
■  White  White

## Backstitch Instructions
All backstitch: DMC #5 Pearl Cotton, White.

## Bead Instructions
• Attach pearl beads with DMC Metallic Floss 5272 White. Refer to "Attaching a Bead" section in General Instructions, page 11, for further assistance, if necessary.

## Heart Glass Treasure Instructions
♡ Attach medium fluted heart Glass Treasure #12208 with DMC Metallic Floss 5272 White in location of heart on the chart.

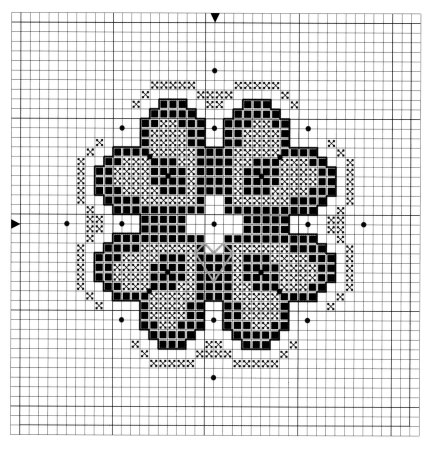

©2002 The DMC Corporation®

# Bride's Purse

### Design by Phyllis Dobbs

*This Bride's Purse sparkles with metallic threads and pearls. The 10-count damask prefinished purse can be stitched in an hour and the bride can use it again and again as an after-five accessory after her wedding day.*

**Cross Stitch:** 1 strand (pearl cotton #5)
or 3 strands embroidery floss
**Backstitch:** 1 strand
**Stitch Counts:** 36 wide x 31 high
**Approximate Finished Size:**
10-count fabric: 3½" wide x 3" high

**Supplies**
- Beautiful Accents™ 10-Count White Damask Prefinished Bride's Purse
- DMC® #5 Pearl Cotton (1 skein each color)
- DMC® 6-Strand Metallic Floss (1 skein each color)
- 40 2.5mm Pearl Beads
- #22 Tapestry Needle

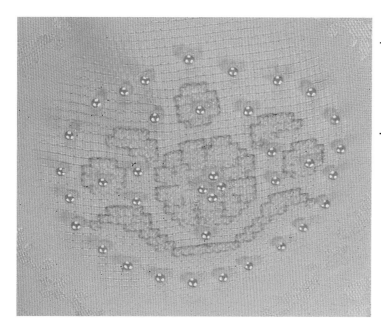

**DMC® 6-Strand Metallic Floss**
✕ 5272 White
**DMC® # 5 Pearl Cotton**
■ White White

## Backstitch Instructions
All backstitch: DMC White White (pearl cotton).

## Bead Instructions
• Attach pearl beads with DMC 5272 White (metallic floss). Refer to "Attaching a Bead" section in General Instructions, page 11, for further assistance, if necessary.

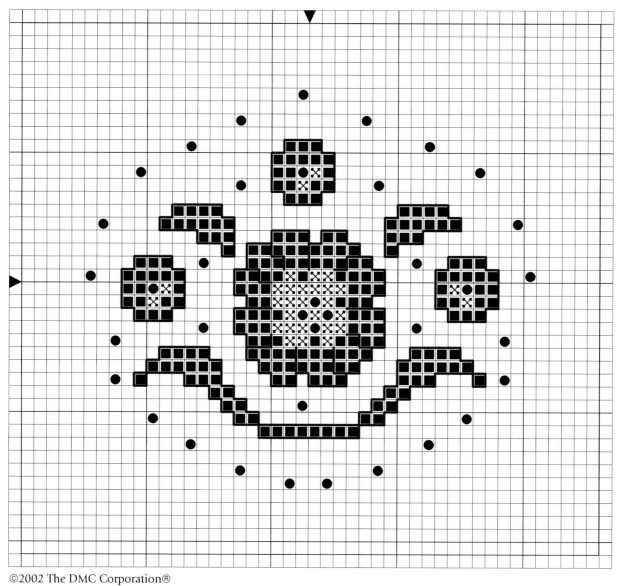

©2002 The DMC Corporation®

# Resources

**Anne Brinkley**
Phone: (520) 888-1462
Lead Crystal Jar #CT4 (page 112).

**Coats & Clark**
Phone: (704) 329-5800
Web site: www.coatsandclark.com
Anchor® 6-Strand Embroidery Floss
and Anchor® Pearl Cotton.
Mail-order source for Anchor:
Herrschners, Inc. (800) 441-0838

**The DMC Corporation**
Web site: www.dmc-usa.com
DMC® 6-Strand Embroidery Floss;
DMC® 6-Strand Rayon Floss;
DMC® 6-Strand Metallic Floss;
DMC® Pearl Cotton; Birthday Bear
(page 29); DMC® 28-count Antique
White Evenweave (page 52); DMC®
25-count Winter White Evenweave
(page 127); DMC® 18-count Sea
Green Aida #964 (page 129);
and DMC® 14-count White Aida
(page 133).
Mail-order source for DMC
Corporation: Herrschners, Inc.
(800) 441-0838

**Charles Craft, Inc.**
Phone: (800) 277-0980
Web site: www.charlescraft.com
14-count White Showcase Towel
(page 19); 14-count White Potholder
(page 68); 14-count White Showcase
Towel (page 68); 14-count White
Aida (page 68); 8.5-count Waste
Canvas (pages 105 and 107);
and 14-count Antique White Aida
(page 123).

**Daniel Enterprises**
Phone: (910) 270-9090
Web site: www.crafterspride.com
Easel-Back Acrylic Frame (pages 17,
23, and 126); 18-count White Vinyl
Weave (pages 17, 23, 41, 120, and
126); Lacy Bookmark #40020W
(page 49); and Switchplate
(page 120).

**Gay Bowles Sales, Inc.**
Phone: (608) 754-9466
Web site: www.millhill.com
Pearl Seed Beads #02001 (page 14);
Red Seed Beads #02063 (page 97);
Red Strawberry Glass Treasure
#12146 (page 97); White Petite
Beads #40479 (page 102);
Crystal Honey Seed Beads #02019
(page 102); Robin Egg Blue Seed
Beads #00143 (page 136); and
Fluted Heart Glass Treasure #12208
(page 139).

**Kreinik Mfg. Co.**
Phone: (410) 281-0040
Web site: www.kreinik.com
Kreinik Braids (pages 14, 35, 45,
and 86-96) and Kreinik High Luster
Blending Filament (pages 112
and 136).
Mail-order source for Kreinik:
Herrschners, Inc. (800) 441-0838

**Sudberry House**
Phone: (860) 739-6951
Web site: www.sudberry.com
Key Rack #10161 (page 50);
Square Oak Box #99188 (page 52);
Cheese Board #95290 (page 68);
and Music Jewelry Box #99451
(page 102).

**Wichelt Imports, Inc.**
Phone: (978) 597-8794
Web site: www.wichelt.com
28-count Champagne Linen
(page 50); 28-count White Linen
(page 105); and 32-count Ivory
Linen (page 112).

**X-Stitch Enterprises, Inc.**
Phone: (512) 989-9383
Web site:
www.x-stitchenterprises.com
Beautiful Accents™ 20-count
Gold/Cream Lugana Album Cover
(page 14); Beautiful Accents™
14-count White Aida Album Cover
(pages 19 and 136); Beautiful
Accents™ 14-count Baby Pillowcase
(page 25); Beautiful Accents™
14-count White Lacy Baby Bib
(page 25); 10-count White Damask
Baby Bib (page 25); Beautiful

Accents™ 14-count White Large Jar
Lacy (page 35); Beautiful Accents™
14-count White Royal Classic Tree
Skirt (page 41); Mouse Pad
(pages 46, 105, and 121); Beautiful
Accents™ 14-count White Lacy Hand
Towel and Washcloth (page 55);
Beautiful Accents™ 10-count White
Tula Table Topper (pages 71 and
104); Beautiful Accents™ 14-count
White Pillow Sham (page 75);
Beautiful Accents™ 14-count White
Standard Pillowcase (page 77);
14-count White Battenburg Doily
(page 77); Plastic Checkbook Cover
(page 105); Beautiful Accents™
10-count White Damask Purse
(pages 105 and 141); Beautiful
Accents™ 7-count Black Country
Aida Shawl (page 115); Sweet
Suspension Frames (page 123); and
Beautiful Accents™ 10-count White
Ring Bearer's Pillow (page 139).

**Zweigart® THE needlework fabric™**
Phone: (732) 562-8888
Web site: www.zweigart.com
White Baby Bib #BG3706/001
(page 19); 16-count White with Blue
Terry Hooded Bath Towel and Mitt
(page 26); 16-count Stitchband with
Red Trim #7003/019 (page 29);
10-count White Damask Largo Table
Topper (page 31); 18-count White-
and-Blue Tannenbaum (page 36);
14-count Royal Blue Stitchband
#7000-5 (page 45); 14-count Ice
Blue Aida (page 46); 14-count
Natural with Hunter Green Stripes
Hearthside Afghan (page 57);
8-count White Cottage Huck Towel
(page 78); 18-count Natural Anne
Cloth Afghan (page 83); 14-count
Royal Blue Westerland Table Topper
(page 99); 36-count White Edinburg
(page 102); Floral Stitchband
#7425-19 (page 97); White
Stitchband #7324-1 (page 111);
and 18-count White Patriotic
Afghan/Ruffled Pillow Sham
(page 117).
Mail-order source for Zweigart pre-
finished items: X-Stitch Enterprises,
Inc. (512) 989-9383

# Contributing Designers

The beautiful projects featured in this book are works from the following creative designers.

*Jane Blum*

*Phyllis Dobbs*

*Laura Doyle*

*Pam Kellogg*

*Roberta Madeleine*

*Ursula Michael*

*Anne Stanton*

*Mike Vickery*

*Lois Winston*

**Jane Blum**
Whale of a Bath Time Set (page 26)

**Phyllis Dobbs**
Birthday Bear (page 29)
Birthday Table Topper (page 31)
Ring Bearer's Pillow(page 139)
Bride's Purse (page 141)

**Laura Doyle**
Wildflower Hand Towel Set (page 55)
God Bless America Switchplate (page 120)

**Pam Kellogg**
Baby Panda Bear Set (page 19)
Baby Blocks Pillowcase and Bib (page 24)
Christmas Tree Jar Lacy (page 35)
I'd Rather Be Fishing Mouse Pad (page 46)
Friend Bookmark (page 49)
Friendship Key Rack (page 50)
Cheese and Grapes Set (page 68)
Blue Roses Bedroom Set (page 71)

Four Seasons Towels (page 78)
Flower-of-the-Month Afghan (page 83)
Poppy and Daisy Table Topper (page 99)
Stitched With Love for You Jewelry Box (floral)
and Floral Table Topper (pages 102 and 104)
Proud To Be An American Mouse Pad
(page 121)

**Roberta Madeleine**
50th Anniversary Album Cover (page 14)
Friendship…a Gift from God (page 52)
Pink Rose Alphabet (page 105)
Mom's Crystal Jar (page 112)
Rose Shawl (page 114)
Wedding Album Cover (page 136)

**Ursula Michael**
50th Anniversary Frame (page 16)
Baby Frame (page 22)
Frosty Folks Pillows (page 36)
Whimsical Santa Tree Skirt
and Ornaments (page 40)
Dad Bookmark (page 45)

Inspirational Wall Hanging (page 97)
Mother Bookmark (page 111)
Patriotic Flag Ornaments (page 123)
Reach For the Stars Graduation Frame
(page 126)

**Anne Stanton**
Stitch Diagrams (pages 10-11)
Waste Canvas Diagram (page 10)

**Mike Vickery**
Sports Afghan (page 57)

**Lois Winston**
Stitched with Love for You Jewelry Box
(lettering) (page 102)
United We Stand Afghan and Pillow
(page 117)
Bar Mitzvah Sampler (page 127)
Bat Mitzvah Sampler (page 129)
Hanukkah/Dreidel Song Sampler (page 131)
Kwanzaa Sampler (page 133)